ONE IN A SERIES FROM THE PUBLISHERS OF *PRE-K TODAY*

LEARNING THROUGH PLAY

MUSIC & MOVEMENT

A Practical Guide for Teaching Young Children

Written by Ellen Booth Church

Foreword by Ella Jenkins

Contributing Writers:

Merle Karnes, Ed.D.

Kathie Spitzley

Constance Ward

Illustrated by Nicole Rubel

With love to my father, Norval Luther Church, and my mother, Francesca Esterly Church,
for creating a home where the joy of spontaneous music and dance
filled our minds and hearts daily.
— ELLEN BOOTH CHURCH

Early Childhood Division Vice President and Publisher
Helen Benham

Art Director
Toby Fox

Production Editor
Katie Lyons

Editor
Jane Schall

Associate Editor
Ilene S. Rosen

Activity Plans written by
Ellen Booth Church,
Lisa Feeney, and Constance Ward

Copyright © 1992 by Scholastic Inc.

Published by:
Scholastic Inc.
Early Childhood Division
730 Broadway
New York, NY 10003

ISBN # 0-590-49249-7
Library of Congress Catalog Number

CONTENTS

LEARNING
AND
GROWING
WITH
MUSIC & MOVEMENT

ACTIVITY
PLANS
FOR TWOS, THREES, FOURS, AND FIVES

Cover Photo: Kate Connell

FOREWORD
MUSIC IS THE WORLD'S LANGUAGE
A CONVERSATION WITH ELLA JENKINS

Q: You are someone who has shared your love of music so creatively with teachers and children all over the world. How does music foster creativity?

A: The thing about music is that you can just start creating your own. And this is what children do all the time. As I share music in one way, they share it in another. Also, the more you work at something, the more you experiment, and the more creative you become. Like writing poetry. First you copy from your favorite poets, and then you say, "Well, I like writing poetry. Now I better set this style aside and see what comes out of me." In particular, if a child is trying a rhythm out and can't quite master it, but creates something interesting, we can follow and recognize it as something that this child has given.

Q: You've performed for and worked with children from so many cultures. Have you been able to help them appreciate their similarities and differences?

A: Yes. In concerts I include various cultures, but not in ways that make anyone feel that he or she is so very different. I might start out saying, "I wonder if anyone can say something, for instance, in Spanish." Then, "I wonder if there are other languages anyone would like to share." Children seem proud to speak other languages, so one child after another comes up and speaks Arabic, Thai, French, German, Cambodian, and so on.

We also listen to different sounds together. For example, a Native American child might get up and in her tribe's language say the number "one," which has two syllables. As the numbers increase, more syllables are added, so I ask her to say the numbers one at a time, and we all repeat them together. It's exciting! Children love to explore and make different sounds.

Another way I introduce cultures without pounding children on the head is by talking about different ways to say "Hello, what's happening?" Sometimes we try "Buenas Dias" or "Bonjour." Right away, they hear and like the way it sounds, and feel "I can do that."

I believe people want to be understood, but too often they don't know how to touch one another's cultures in peaceful ways. And that's why it's so important for those of us who work with children not to use stereotypes. Children are going to get whatever they're going to get — stereotyped jokes, chants like "Eenie-Meenie-Miney-Mo." They've been out there for years. But they shouldn't get them from us.

Q: Where does music fit it? How does it make things special?

A: Most people, children and adults, like music — something that makes them close their eyes and listen quietly, tap their feet, or snap their fingers. When they get comfortable, they share. Some children don't respond to loud music; some love music whether we think so or not. But variety is always important.

It's also important to not get caught up in your voice or think that you're not a good singer. Use tapes. Just remember that it's terribly important to monitor what children listen to. Music is everywhere. We have to catch it wherever it is and be selective in how we share it with children.

Q: Do you bring instruments with you from place to place?

A: Instruments and sometimes songs, sometimes phrases or rhythms, and sometimes I'll write a song from experiences and words that people share with me. I went to the Great Wall once on a little train, and the place where we got off the train was called Pataliang. There were a lot of children singing on the train so I listened to their song, and wrote one called "The Train to Pataliang." Now I share the song *and* the experience.

Q: What advice would you like to offer?

A: Children, especially young ones, need to get acquainted with the sounds their bodies can make — clapping hands, snapping fingers, beating chests, slapping thighs, tapping knees. Each movement has a different tone, a different sound. With music, that's what you work with — sounds, tones, and rhythms.

After children feel at ease with their bodies, give small groups rhythm sticks and let each child develop his or her sense of rhythm. Sometimes we get children into very stylistic movements, such as ballet, before they're really ready. The natural rhythm of childhood is hopping, skipping, jumping, walking. I've never seen a child skipping down the street with a frown.

Then there are hand drums, tambourines, maracas, claves, and bells of different types to explore one by one. So you have a variety of sounds and tones, some from your bodies, and some from a variety of instruments children play in their own ways.

Q: What about using recorded music?

A: Use it as a complement rather than by itself. If you have a listening period, have a participation time. It's contrast. If you don't have contrast, your day will be very dull — for everyone.

Q: Are there any thoughts you'd like to leave us with?

A: I'd like to share an old musician's union phrase: "Keep music alive!" It's something we all can get into, and a part of our cultures. It's something we should learn about others.

"Let us first teach little children to breathe, to vibrate, to feel, and to become one with the general harmony and movement of nature. Let us first produce a beautiful human being, a dancing child."

— *Isadora Duncan*

FOSTERING SPONTANEOUS MUSIC & MOVEMENT

We live in a musical, rhythmic world. Sounds, patterns, and movement are all around us. The sound of the rain on the roof and the rhythm of the changing days and seasons spark our senses and at the same time create a natural order. Think about it: The sound and rhythm of our own breathing is essential to life! Truly, music and movement are fundamental to all beings.

Accordingly, spontaneous music and movement are vital to the creative educational process. In a sense, they are a microcosm of the full spectrum of education. Through spontaneous music and movement, we enable the whole child to grow emotionally, creatively, socially, and cognitively. As we support children's innate desire to create, we build on their natural curiosities, sparking imaginations and opening avenues for free expression.

It is our responsibility as important adults in children's lives to protect and nurture their interests and abilities in life-affirming ways. In the process, we must remember that the focal point of teaching is not the curriculum or the activity, but the child.

SPONTANEOUS MUSIC: THE SPARK WITHIN

There is a busy hum to the day. Among the sounds of children working and playing, another sound emerges. Faint at first, it slowly builds into full voice. Someone is singing! Near the clay table you can hear a musical "Push, push, push; squish, squish, squish; pat, pat, pat." It's a child's song with its own special tune.

And, as she works the clay, the tune, rhythm, and lyrics fit her actions. Eventually other children come over, pick up pieces of clay, and join in the song. At first the "songwriter" leads, but the other children soon add their own creative energy to make a glorious, spontaneous composition!

The children in this scenario know the joy of spontaneous music — a magical process that comes from a place deep inside. The music may consist of elements of tunes children have heard before, or entirely new ones. Whatever the essence, the musical experience is of their own design, created without adult prompting or direction. What could be more creative?

This particular kind of music making is an important part of early childhood. Rather than telling children what to do or how to do it — rather than guiding their experiences by saying, "Let's make music like a bird," or, "Sound like a train" — teachers can provide supportive settings in which children feel free to invent their own sounds, tunes, and lyrics. Based on their own ideas, children will own the experience and the music.

As you know, a well-rounded early childhood setting needs to offer children a balance between spontaneous and guided musical experiences. Of course, children enjoy singing familiar songs, but it is equally important to provide them with opportunities that encourage their individual spontaneity. These two types of musical experience come from different sources and, in turn, address different areas of children's development.

When we teach children music, we use external stimuli such as a new song, fingerplay, or chant. A child hears the song and learns it through repeated practice. On the other hand, spontaneous music is internal, coming from a personal spark that urges the child to put his or her feelings, thoughts, or actions into song. Whether it's the delight of spotting a bright red bird outside the window, the exhilaration of gliding high on a swing, or a rush of feeling about an upcoming party, the stimulus ignites self-creation. This rich form of self-expression is part of what young children do every day!

Like speaking, drawing, writing, and pretending, self-created music making provides an avenue for children to express how they feel and what they are thinking, seeing, and doing.

Just as we all learned to talk by

talking, children learn to sing their own songs by singing them. When they feel a part of an environment that supports spontaneity, they experiment. Our goal is to help children see themselves as musicians, just as we want them to scc themselves as artists. If we approach music in much the same way we do art, opening all doors to creativity, we encourage children to continually express themselves in their own ways.

SPONTANEOUS MOVEMENT: FEELING THE BEAT

Music naturally makes children want to move, and when it is their own music, the magic intensifies! Watch as children find a beat they've created so irresistible that they start tapping their toes, clapping their hands, and swinging their hips. Just as we want to support the natural music that emerges from within, we also want to support children's natural movement. Early childhood is not a time to show children how to move or to limit their ways of moving.

Creative movement is so much more than physical exercise. Coming from deep inside, it is a total involvement of heart, soul, limbs, and senses. Your openness to this type of letting go encourages children to express whatever they're feeling through their bodies, not only fostering creative development but also helping children feel good about themselves.

All people, especially children, have a desire to create. By encouraging children to express their movements spontaneously, you provide them with opportunities to create not just with their minds and hands, but also with their whole bodies. After finally mastering walking and climbing, it is a wonderful treat for children to be encouraged to "play" with the ways they move.

Also, young children are intrigued with movement — how things, people, and animals move. Have you ever seen a child swinging on the monkey bars while watching a leaf sway in the breeze? Or "trying on" the movement of an animal? So much is happening in the event. Besides the opportunity to freely express themselves, children learn about balance, motion, and experimentation as they see what happens when they move a certain way and lose their balance. This causes them to construct their own knowledge about the physical world. It is a natural fascination we can support and encourage.

Too often children are asked to "move like horses" or "pretend they are trees in the wind." This creates a problem because children have limited prior knowledge or experience and are often led to believe that there is a "right" way to move. But when they innately imitate an animal or move like something that catches their eye in their environment, they are basing their movcment on concrete experiences and inner motivation.

You can support these individual dances and movements by letting children know there is no one *right* way. Rather than asking everyone to copy a particular child's movements (or yours), show that you appreciate the movements of each person. You might exclaim, "Look at all the different ways our bodies are going. Each one of us is moving in a special way." In this way, children know you do not have a preconceived notion in mind and you value their creativity.

If a spontaneous song and dance begin in a crowded area, allow children to become involved and develop the experience. Then help them find a larger space to continue. By doing this, you let them know that you value what they are doing and you want them to continue safely. Often this will encourage children to develop their music and movement even further. Don't be afraid of a little noise and commotion. Remember that this is one more way young children can truly express — and keep alive — that spark within.

YOUR EARLY EXPERIENCES

We all start life deeply involved with music and movement. Truly, every baby is a singer and dancer moving to his or her own rhythm, cooing and gurgling beautiful songs. Put on some music and a baby will start to move and sing, no reservations, no embarrassment.

At some point in our growing years some of us lose this freedom of expression. Suddenly there is a "right way" to sing or dance because we feel that free expression must fit a standard or mold. Perhaps it happened with family members or teachers. Often it happens in grade school where music is taught by a specialist who made performance more important than process.

All people are singers and dancers, just as they were when they were babies. When music and movement are approached from a place of creative expression, we all can feel successful. When we remember that there is no one right way, we can look inside and find the child who loved to make up songs and move around the room — the child who knows how to make music and movement an expression of joy and life!

AGES & STAGES
OF MUSIC & MOVEMENT DEVELOPMENT

The way children engage in music and movement activities depends not only on their experiences, but on their ages and developmental levels. Use these guidelines as you think about music and movement experiences, to help you gauge the various abilities and interests in your group.

TWO-YEAR-OLDS MAY:

■ use their bodies, especially their arms, in response to music, making primarily up-and-down movements. But they also delight in showing off newly developed movement abilities such as running, galloping, and jumping rhythmically.

■ experiment with simple words and syllables and repeat them in rhythmic patterns.

■ delight in listening to songs sung just for them. They may watch your face, especially your mouth, as you sing.

■ respond to familiar songs and want to hear them over and over. Individual children might sing parts of songs, but rarely sing with a group.

■ at times seem more interested in the motions that go with a song than in actually singing it.

■ like to tap their own rhythms and use instruments that they can strike or strike with, such as drums and rhythm sticks.

You can help by:
■ offering safe spaces for children to experiment with expressive movement.

■ avoiding large-group music and movement activities.

■ creating a music-rich environment for your children that exposes them to a wide variety of sounds, tempos, and styles.

■ making up and singing simple, spontaneous songs throughout the day that use a few repetitive notes and words to express a feeling or action.

■ providing one-to-one opportunities to experiment with both vocal and rhythmic sounds.

THREE-YEAR-OLDS MAY:

■ move expressively with more fluid motion, using their arms in circular and linear fashions.

■ like to listen to music that is either loud or very active. Threes may dance spontaneously in response to music, but usually prefer not to be noticed.

■ sing favorites in small groups — repetitive songs and chants with hand motions. They often choose either to sing or move, but not both.

■ enjoy pretend or silly songs that make them laugh.

■ make up their own songs that become more elaborate as language abilities mature.

You can help by:
■ providing lively music and a safe space that encourages children to use active, large motions including running and jumping.

■ observing children's spontaneous

dances without calling attention to them.

■ matching your singing with theirs, following their lead. Threes aren't necessarily ready to pay attention to pitch and shouldn't be expected to do so.

■ creating a supportive environment for individual experimentation with sound and movement. Children may form their own small groups, but keep large group activities to a minimum.

FOUR-YEAR-OLDS MAY:

■ show a desire to "perform" their movements and songs for adults and other children.

■ enjoy listening to songs, records, and stories. Fours particularly like songs in which they can participate by chanting, singing, or doing a motion.

■ become more interested in singing with a group. They learn fingerplays, simple songs, and chants easily now and may be able to repeat them from memory.

■ invent new lyrics to favorite songs, often using silly or made-up words.

■ repeat and sustain a rhythmic beat without assistance, naturally tapping along to create and play their own rhythms.

You can help by:

■ providing plenty of opportunities for expressive movement and movement games, and offering props for children's experimentation.

■ supporting children's performances without interfering, and being prepared to turn your attention elsewhere if a child suddenly becomes shy.

■ continually offering opportunities for open-ended *group* music and movement activities, though some fours will choose not to participate.

■ introducing personalized songs the group can add lyrics to, such as "Old MacDonald." Fours also love songs that include their names.

■ playing follow-the-leader-type

rhythm and movement games and encouraging children to take turns being the leader using their own spontaneous sounds, rhythms, and motions.

FIVE-YEAR-OLDS MAY:

■ have lots of creative energy!

■ show an interest in using props for movement and dramatization.

■ enthusiastically participate in large-group singing and movement. They are more interested in — and more able to sing — conventional songs, but still enjoy creating their own words and motions.

■ show a greater interest in listening activities — new music and sounds, as well as simple listening games.

■ be fascinated by rhythm instruments, but are often more interested in making noise than in listening to the music they're creating.

You can help by:

■ being understanding of children's need to make noise and use large motions. Provide appropriate space, time, and props.

■ choosing songs with a wider pitch range and less repetitive lyrics. Fives enjoy songs with a chorus and a changing set of verses.

■ organizing group singing and movement times every day. Invite children to suggest songs to sing. Support their efforts to create "innovative" lyrics.

■ providing varied listening opportunities with different styles of music and with story records such as "Beauty and the Beast" or "Peter and the Wolf."

■ developing an awareness of the world of sounds by playing listening and imitating games.

■ providing a variety of instruments and inviting children to find all the different sounds they can make, as well as leaving them plenty of time to explore on their own.

YOUR ROLE

Rather than being an instructor or teacher, your role in fostering spontaneous expression is that of supporter and facilitator. Much like an orchestra conductor who doesn't play the instruments or write the music, you are an artist who facilitates a combination of natural energies. And like a conductor, rather than lead or control, you create a supportive environment, following children's leads and respecting and nurturing their free expression.

SEEING YOURSELF AS A MUSICIAN AND DANCER

One of the first steps in understanding your role is to experiment with music and movement yourself. After all, it's difficult to encourage children's free expression if you feel restrained or blocked yourself. There are some simple ways you can do this without feeling self-conscious. Sing along with the car radio, or, better yet, make up sounds to go with the car sounds you hear, then spin them into a tune. Many of us sing in the shower, but usually songs we know. Stop and listen for a minute. Does the sound of the water make a tune? Try humming along with it. Create a tune for cooking dinner, going shopping, even chopping wood. You might be surprised how quickly these ditties come to mind once you get started — and they make your work go faster, too.

Take time to notice the sounds in your life. You already make sounds every day. Listen and extend them in the same ways children do. Do you make a sound when you pick something up? How about when you sit down quickly? Do you make a sound when you are thinking? Repeat it, add to it, and see where it goes. Soon you'll be making more sounds, and a little phrase or tune will emerge. This is a beginning of your own spontaneous music.

Expand on natural movements in your life and you've created a spontaneous dance. While driving the car do you ever tap you fingers to the radio? That's a start. Extend it, tap somewhere else, wiggle your fingers, change the rhythm, add an arm motion — you're involved in a dance.

Through experimenting with your own spontaneous music and movements, you can gain understanding of how to facilitate young children's experiences. Plus, by breaking down our own walls of convention, we not only see how to encourage children, but also add enjoyment to our lives.

FOLLOWING CHILDREN'S LEADS

As you know, children create their own world of music and movement. They use the rich soil of their life experiences to grow a vast garden of delights. Who are we to tell them how their music should sound or their dances should look?

One important part of your role as a facilitator is to continually let children know that you respect their ability to construct experiences based on their individual knowledge and understanding. One way to do this is to tune in to children and follow their lead. In doing so, we acknowledge them as musicians and dancers. When we encourage children to be leaders, we assure them that their ideas are valid and supported. This support helps children to expand on what they know and feel safe with — experimenting with new, perhaps more risky sounds and movements. Of course, a wonder-

Photo: Kate Connell

ful part of all this growth is enhanced self-esteem — children seeing themselves as successful, contributing members of a group.

WATCHING & LISTENING

Think of children's spontaneous music and movement as a hands-off activity for adults. In other words, we can learn so much when we take the time to observe and listen to children's music making. How is the child expressing his or her own music or movement? Is she using parts of familiar tunes (often commercials!) to create a song or is she making up a completely new tune? Is she creating an elaboration of familiar lyrics? Are the movements based on a sound or motion she is currently observing? This information tells you how each child is constructing the experience. Let it be a doorway into understanding each individual's thinking. Use this information to facilitate experiences in the future.

ACKNOWLEDGING

Most children like to be noticed in supportive and gentle ways. Unless you know that a particular child would prefer to be by herself, wait until she has sung freely for a while and then make a comment: "Nice song." If appropriate, add, "Can I sing it, too?" Sing along just the way the child is singing. Never lead the song away from itself. Remember, if there are going to be any changes, they need to come from the child. Sometimes just a smile or a nod is all that's needed to tell a child that you support her activity. Some children don't even realize they are making up a song or a dance because it's so natural and spontaneous. When you quietly acknowledge these events, you help children become aware of what they are doing in a supportive way.

OFFERING ASSISTANCE

Sometimes it's appropriate to help children elaborate. For example, you might offer to tape-record a group song that sprang up during play in the block corner. (Most children love to hear their songs played back and will use the recording process as inspiration to embellish.) You also might suggest adding rhythm instruments. Older children often like to have the lyrics of their songs written down. And when children are creating a spontaneous dance you might bring out the movement prop box so they can choose their own props to add to their motions. Or suggest they find a special place in the room for creating their dance.

CREATING A SHARING ENVIRONMENT

Make time for children to share their music and movement by inviting but never forcing them. Some like to "perform" and welcome opportunities to show off their newest work in a nonjudgmental atmosphere where everyone's song or dance is a masterpiece. Group sharing can encourage children who are feeling shy to take risks which they might not have tried by themselves. The effect can become circular when group support empowers children who might not experiment on their own to take new initiative.

MODELING

Your delight in spontaneous music and movement provides an important model and contributes greatly to building a music- and movement-rich environment. Besides the usual cleanup-time song, make up songs all day long — taking attendance, zipping up coats, cleaning up a spill. And remember, for getting children's attention, nothing works better than a new song! Vary songs frequently so music doesn't become routine. Everyday events and activities — stirring the muffin batter, sorting buttons, hammering at the workbench — can turn into original tunes or familiar ones, adding your own words. Try including fun facts about your children and yourself, singing questions and encouraging children to sing their responses.

And how about walking to the playground? Move in different ways and children will surely join in. Your free expressive movements invite everyone to invent new ways to move. You might say, "How can we leave circle time in a new way? Make up a way other than walking to move?"

ENRICHING

Because it's important to always reinforce the concept that there is no one right way, you'll want to expose children to a wide variety of sounds and styles. Some music may sound odd or strange at first, but children generally have little difficulty developing new appreciation, especially with your supportive lead. Playing music just for everyone's listening pleasure doesn't mean formal music appreciation times, but opportunities for children to hear music and tune in to its nuances. Use different styles of music as accompaniments to various activities. For example, if you are pounding nails, do it to a salsa beat; or glide around together to some lovely waltzes. However, always remember: It is important that music not just become part of the background of the day — then you will be teaching children to ignore music, rather then enjoy it.

Much the same holds true for movement activities. By encouraging children to move in all sorts of ways and exposing them to many different forms of dancing — through pictures, books, and, if possible, live demonstrations — you will keep them from narrowly defining what dance is. At the same time, you'll allow them the latitude to consider all ways of moving as dance, and begin to lay a foundation for an acceptance and appreciation of differences.

Music & Movement in
Family Day-Care Homes

"Bumpity bump, bumpity bump." Two two-year-olds are chanting as they bump their backsides against the furniture in syncopation. Most homes are great environments to discover spontaneous music. Convenient pathways from kitchen to dining room to living room are quickly discovered as spontaneous bands march along. And a supportive adult who joins in the fun helps reserve space for the slower movers in the multiage group.

Here are tips to keep in mind as you encourage spontaneous music and movement in your multiage group:

▪ Play a variety of music during play times. Use the richness of children's varying backgrounds and cultural experiences as a resource for music and movement activities. (Remember that respecting these differences allows children to feel good about their uniqueness and encourages them to value this quality in others.)

▪ Encourage children's music as they go about the tasks within your home. For instance, a young three might set the table, tapping a beat with unbreakable plates and singing his original song: "I'm a marching band, I'm a marching band." Or you might help older children rise from a short rest time with, "Heigh ho, heigh ho, it's time for jobs, you know. We'll wipe the chairs and sweep the stairs, heigh ho, heigh ho."

▪ Keep objects around that can add to children's musical experiences. An empty gallon milk jug and a wooden spoon make a great sound together. Buttons in a sealed plastic bottle are terrific rattlers. Rubber bands around a tissue box can simulate a guitar, especially when you add a small wooden "bridge." An empty toilet-paper roll with waxed paper on one end vibrates like a kazoo. Dried gourds with seeds, and ice cream sticks inserted in taped boxes filled with beans or stones, allow children to create their own sounds. Sticks bang together, keys jingle, bolts clang — keeping children's rhythms and beats.

▪ Take your orchestra into the neighborhood. Use empty pickle barrels, plastic water bottles, and crates to carry instruments. Sing and march up and down your street. The activity will keep your group together. Just slow down to the pace of the youngest participants while you investigate neighborhood happenings such as tree pruning, sidewalk replacement, and road repairs.

▪ As you hammer, sing about hammering; as you stir, sing about stirring. You'll soon find older children telling stories to younger ones that have their own special rhythms and songs, too.

▪ Set clear limits for what you consider safe in your environment. If children may not jump on the couch, locate a place where it is safe and okay to jump. Monitor use of rhythm sticks, making sure an adult is always close by when they are in use. Make sure children have enough space to march and/or dance. Remember, even doorknobs are just the right height for a four-year-old to bump an ear.

▪ Allow time for things to unfold leisurely so children's spontaneity has a chance. For example, children who do not feel hurried will often sing a song on their way from cleanup to the snack table.

▪ Never forget: To be spontaneous in their expressions, children need to feel successful in their environments.

Kathie Spitzley, a family day-care provider in Holland, Michigan, for 10 years, is accredited by the National Association of Family Day Care.

MUSIC WITH YOUNG CHILDREN

How many of us have felt we can't sing very well? Why is that? Where did that thinking begin? As you know, we often develop opinions of ourselves at very young ages. Overemphasis on structured music and getting it "right" can foster these negative points of view. Children who have difficulty staying with a song or feeling a particular rhythm may feel musically inadequate. If your setting doesn't encourage spontaneous musical experiences, these children can get the feeling that they aren't musical, that their own music doesn't sound like "real" music, and that they can't sing.

However, sharing music from many cultures — tunes with interesting scales, tones, rhythms, instruments, and unusual-sounding words — is one way to maintain openness to and appreciation of variety. The longer you listen with a positive ear, the more unique and special the music becomes. Think of your children's own music in the same way, valuing the interesting nuances. Celebrate these nuances with your children, pointing out interesting sounds rather than conveying an attitude that there is a "right" way to sound.

And, even if you think you can't sing, try! Remember, you are a very important model and, in general, young children view adults' singing as wonderful no matter how it may sound to other adults. Perhaps this is because they haven't defined music narrowly yet!

Always remember that you don't have to be a musician to create wonderful music experiences for young children. Traditionally, early childhood teachers have felt that they needed to know how to play the piano, guitar, or Autoharp. Yet we have the most valuable instrument of

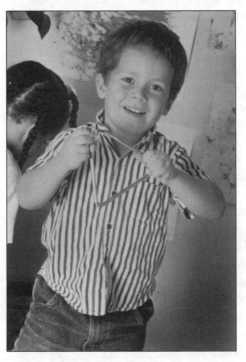

all — our voices! This is where children's own spontaneous music begins and it is the same for adults. With our voices we can experiment with sounds, rhythms, melodies, and beats — the basics of music. After all, our voices are natural instruments which we all experimented with as infants and young children. The idea is to keep this experimentation going.

Haven't most of us sung to an infant, particularly when we thought no one was listening? And how do infants react? They love it! They don't cringe if we're not perfectly in tune. They usually smile, coo, and probably answer back.

So starting right now, consider yourself a natural musician. Sing a spontaneous song, hum a tune, make music an even greater part of your life. If it still feels uncomfortable, try chanting a song and asking children for their help. You might ask, "Do you know a tune for these words?" Or try humming or singing a few notes of a familiar song and ask children to join in. They enjoy opportunities to take the lead. Re-

member, you are your own worst critic. Your courage to sing spontaneously inspires children to let their creativity soar.

CREATING A BALANCED APPROACH TO MUSIC EXPERIENCES

In planning music experiences, you need to consider a balance between spontaneous and guided music activities. While the activities need to spring from child-created musical situations, guided activities need to be limited in number and flexible in nature. The amount of each will vary according to developmental levels (see "Ages & Stages," page 8), with older children engaging in more group and guided activities than younger ones. Keep your plans flexible, and make one of your goals to be open to teachable moments — when it is more important to follow children's leads than to complete what might be in your plan book.

One way to be sure you are providing a balanced approach is to remember that children learn best when they are involved — when a topic of interest is modeled and shared, while children are allowed to experiment and explore independently. The combination of these approaches provides a complete storehouse of experiences from which a child can draw. When this model is applied to music, it means that we provide music activities *for* children, *with* children, and *by* children.

MUSIC FOR CHILDREN

Musical experiences *for* children include opportunities for them to see and hear others creating their own spontaneous music. Singing your own songs, humming a tune, mak-

HOW TO CHOOSE GOOD MUSIC FOR CHILDREN

There are many recordings available for young children. Some are excellent; others may have appropriate songs mixed with inappropriate ones. This means it's important to listen to entire recordings before you play them for your group. (You can always choose specific songs to share.) Here are other important considerations to think about:

▼ **Find music that is non-directive.** Songs that tell children how to move obviously limit their choices. Look for music that encourages they to make their own interpretations and experiment freely.

▼ **Choose a wide variety.** There are limitless kinds of music to share! Jazz, folk, rock, country, new age, reggae, and, of course, classical, are just some of the kinds of music you can enjoy together. Be sure to include lots of music without lyrics to help children tune in to instruments and their sounds.

▼ **Enjoy music from many cultures.** These selections broaden children's musical awareness and often inspire them to create their own songs and music. Bagpipes, steel drums, maracas, and castanets are just the beginning of musical experiences from around the world.

▼ **Listen carefully to lyrics.** When you do play music that includes words, take time to focus beforehand on whether the lyrics promote or encourage any stereotypes about age, race, gender, or abilities. Take care that the songs children listen to are age-appropriate as well as fun.

ing up songs for transitions, and musically describing daily events are all excellent models for children's own spontaneous music without being restrictive or prescriptive in nature.

Listening

Listening to a variety of music, both live and recorded, is another form of music *for* children. Many children are fascinated by different instruments and will listen attentively for short periods of time. So invite parents, older children, and friends to share their singing or an instrument with your group. (Beforehand, ask the visitor if there is a way children can safely experiment with the instrument themselves.) Children do not forget these types of experiences with live music, and they often inspire future instrumentalists!

Listening activities can be important "music *for* children" events. Some of us may have terrible memories of music appreciation classes we had to endure in school. The problem was that those classes were passive experiences with music. Young children are active listeners. They need to be able to respond to music with movement, creative dance, clapping, or playing rhythm instruments. Choose good music from a variety of sources (see "How to Choose Good Music for Children," left). Invite families to not only share their own musical abilities, but their favorite recordings. In this way, you can be sure to provide some music that is familiar while introducing new musical sounds. Remember, as you show that you value all music equally, you are supporting each child's own prior experiences.

Create a comfortable atmosphere for listening with carpets or pillows so children can *choose* to listen with relaxed attention. For the most part, listening for pure enjoyment is satisfactory to young children for only short periods of time. Many need a reason for listening, and also need to

understand what they are listening for. You might ask children to listen for a particular instrumental sound, a beat, or a change in feeling. You can also encourage children to respond to music with art materials, movements, and even their own sounds.

Many pieces of music suggest a story. *Fantasia* by Walt Disney is an excellent example of the pictures or stories music can create in our minds. *Small and limited* sections of this movie (video) are excellent for music listening activities. From this, children may be inspired to envision stories or pictures as they listen to other music. Try reading *I See a Song* by Eric Carle (Thomas Y. Crowell) for a wonderful, wordless picture-story approach to the art of listening to music. Look for the books based on old favorite tunes that are now being published, such as *Old MacDonald* by Carol Jones (Creative Edge), *The Wheels on the Bus* by Maryann Kovalski (Gryphon House), and *Morningtown Ride* by Malvina Reynolds (Turn-the-Page Press).

MUSIC WITH CHILDREN

Shared musical experiences are an essential part of a balanced approach. However, within these shared experiences there needs to be both spontaneous and planned musical activities. As always, the starting place and the emphasis are on open-ended spontaneous events. These are opportunities to join in children's own improvised songs — playing with a child-created rhythm or chant — and support their own musical events.

This means that most often children are the originators of the activity, yet sometimes we are the initiators of musical experiences. Remember to initiate without controlling, restricting, or judging. Then you will be creating an open, supportive atmosphere for child involvement. There are times when group sing-alongs are appropriate, and when choosing and introducing a new song just feels right. The following are guidelines to consider in choosing new songs and presenting them in ways that are open-ended and child-centered.

What to Look for in Selecting Songs

There are certain elements that make songs appropriate for use with young children. Choose songs that:
- are short in length
- have few words or use repetitive lyrics
- use a limited note range
- use rhythmic and melodic repetition
- move melodically in steps instead of jumping around the scale
- have content that involves, amuses, and/or excites children
- establish a close connection between the words and the musical phrase.

Introducing a New Song

When you introduce a new song you open a magical doorway for children. It is important that this experience be inviting, interesting, and free from pressure for participation or perfection. Here are a few suggestions to consider:
- Choose a song you like so that you can introduce it with enthusiasm.
- Begin by humming the song during activities, inviting children to hum along, too.
- On successive days, add words to the song as you informally sing it during the day.
- Use a visual prop to introduce and illustrate the song or topic, such as a puppet, stuffed animal, photograph, picture, or book.
- Memorize the song so that you do not have to look at the music and can sing it with expression.
- Sing the song straight through to the end, using appropriate rhythm and tempo.
- Make eye contact with the children. The children will be watching your face, so be dramatic!
- Invite children to clap or tap along while you sing.
- Repeat the song several times so

that children can join in when they feel comfortable. Sing the song informally and formally over the next several days and weeks so children can become familiar with it.
- If appropriate, add hand motions to dramatize the song. Invite children to create movements to further dramatize the content.
- Sing softly so that your voice does not overpower or lead the children too much. Inviting children to "help you sing the song" encourages them to sing out.

MUSIC BY CHILDREN

The third and most important approach to music experiences with young children is their own independent musical expression. The necessity of providing opportunities to create spontaneous music has been discussed in the section "Fostering Spontaneous Music & Movement." Supporting children's improvisations with sound, melody, and tempo establishes them as true music makers. What about children's rhythmic improvisations? Let's take a look at how to encourage them to experiment with rhythm instruments.

Using Rhythm Instruments Open-endedly

Spontaneous music naturally leads to improvising with instruments. Rather than restricting children to marching or accompanying a rhythmic record, which can tend to encourage children to see instruments as simply noisemakers, help them understand the full range of sound possibilities. Give everyone time to experiment freely. Leave a box of instruments near your record or tape player. (See "Setting Up," page 23.) During free play, put on some music and let children decide whether they'd like to add accompaniment. Vary the types and styles of music on different days, and set up the area so children can choose the music themselves.

Another time, you might choose an

instrument and ask, "How many different sounds do you think we can make with this instrument? Can you make a quiet sound? A sad sound? A happy sound? A scary sound?" Choose another instrument and try again. Then take a minute to talk about the differences. Leave the instruments out so children can create their own music, perhaps adding words or a collection of their own sounds that seem to fit the instrumental ones. Add a few yourself!

You might also create a totally improvisational band, using gadgets as instruments. (Safe kitchen tools work well because they can make so many different types of sounds.) Offer a variety, let children create the sounds, and make up a song to go along.

When you feel your children's joy as they create something totally unique and beautiful in its own right, you are on your way to being an effective facilitator of children's music. This is the time when the best teaching is the least teaching — when you look inside yourself and see and feel a musical spark aglow. It's in all of us. Release it, feed it, and let the music soar!

Making Rhythm Instruments for Children

Part of the fun of using instruments with young children is making them yourself! Use sturdy materials that will stand up to lots of active use by three-, four-, and five-year-olds. Make sure all pieces are safe for children and attached securely. Here are a few suggestion to get you started.

Sandpaper Blocks — Thoroughly sand two three- by five-inch pieces of wood. Then cut pieces of fine-grain sandpaper large enough to cover the blocks. Wrap the sandpaper around the sides of the blocks widthwise and attach using a staple gun and/or heavy-duty glue. You can leave the wood tops of the blocks plain or decorate them with permanent marking pens.

Rhythm Sticks — Saw thick wooden dowels or broom handles into matching lengths about 12 inches long. Sandpaper the edges and ends so there are no rough spots. Leave plain, varnish, or even paint.

Tambourines — For a great variation, string pieces of telephone wire or other plastic-coated wire through several large bells. Then twist the wires at intervals around an embroidery hoop. Next, cover the wires by wrapping heavy yarn around the hoop in a blanket stitch. Tie the end of the yarn in a knot around the hoop.

Wrist Bells — Cut lengths of wide, dark-colored elastic so they'll fit loosely and comfortably around children's wrists. Use heavy blanket or rug thread to securely sew at least four small bells along each one. Then sew the ends together to form a circle.

Drums — These can be a little more difficult to make, but the results are worth it. *Smoothly* cut out both ends of a coffee can. Now cut two circles out of an opened inner tube to make the top and bottom. (Each circle should be three inches wider than the can openings.) Cut or punch six to eight holes along the edges of the circles. Stretch one circle over each open end of the can and connect them by lacing up and down the drum using plastic or sturdy cotton lacing. Once you've laced the ends loosely all around, go back and tighten as much as possible.

MUSIC WITH
INFANTS & TODDLERS

Spontaneous music has a special and important place in the lives of very young children. Babies innately create their own songs as they coo and gurgle, experimenting with sounds and tones. This is not just the beginning of talking, but the beginning of singing and music making. Very young children will create songs to accompany their actions or to express their feelings or needs. Listen closely and you'll hear the difference between a happy song and a sad one.

Most adults naturally support this type of early music making. How many times have you noticed yourself echoing back a little sound to the tune a baby is making? This is exactly what these young children need us to do. Through "echo singing" we reflect their songs, and children hear us, feeling supported as it all becomes a delightful game. As the child hears you respond, he or she creates more music and "tests" your ability to respond in kind. Through this process, children feel a sense of power. They are the leaders.

Put everyday events into song. Make up simple songs for diaper changing, eating, swinging, even tickling! Create new ones frequently. As you probably already know, young children love hearing songs and often will respond positively when an activity is put to music. Plus, you are modeling the joy of singing throughout the day.

Remember, too, to play *good* music for everyone's listening pleasure. Rather than "cutesy" baby records recorded in high,

shrill voices, choose music with a wide variety of instrumental styles and soothing natural voices. At the same time, remember that children have varying degrees of sensitivity to sound, and some will prefer quiet. Take time to get to know children's preferences as you offer music in different styles and moods.

SING A SONG WITH ME

Both infants and toddlers love to be sung to. Lullabies, simple childhood melodies, and participation songs have never lost their appeal. Share your own favorites, too, because children pick up on your enjoyment.

Keep in mind that many toddlers love repetition in songs. In fact, you'll find they request the same tune again and again many times before they begin to sing it themselves. Toddlers also love to hear their names in the songs you sing and are excited to recognize the names of others.

I CAN MAKE MUSIC!

The first musical instrument very young children learn to play is themselves. Clapping their hands, tapping their toes, making noises with their mouths, and banging one toy against another or the floor form the foundations for many early musical experiences. Make sure you allow time for play.

Toddlers also like experimenting with rhythm instruments, particularly any that can be banged or struck. Although this activity calls for careful supervision, give your toddlers time to play with short rhythm sticks, jingle and hand bells, tambourines, and cymbals. (Also provide plenty of space to prevent collisions.) Remember, toddlers won't be able to keep instruments out of their mouths so select safe, durable ones, and plan to sanitize them after each use.

LISTENING TO MUSIC

You'll find a wide variety of good children's music available. Also provide unbreakable music boxes and one or two durable child-proof tape players so individual children can enjoy their favorite tunes. Use your tape player to bring music into different areas of your room and outdoors.

Look for music that will allow you to enjoy different styles. Classical, contemporary, jazz, and folk are only some of the many kinds of music that create a variety of moods and feelings. This variety of tone and rhythm exposes children to the richness of music, as well as to a wealth of musical heritage.

MOVEMENT
WITH YOUNG CHILDREN

*I*t 's free-play time. At the sink a few children, having washed their hands, remain nearby, fascinated with the "drip, drip, drip" of the faucet. One child starts tapping his feet in time with the drips while another hops to the rhythm. Walking by, still another child begins to clap, and a spontaneous "dance" is created! After observing for a while, their teacher adds her encouragement by echoing the movements with a drum beat. One child says, "Look, I can bounce like dripping water." Others join in and soon a group of children are all creating their own movements.

Our role, as facilitators of creative spontaneous movement, is to help make these activities joyful experiences as children become aware of all the ways they can express themselves through their bodies. We can reinforce this natural expression by encouraging them to experiment. We can build self-esteem by showing them that we value their movement play. Most importantly, we can help each child be a leader of his or her own "dance" by recognizing that movement is not something children need to be taught (they know how) and remembering that their innate, spontaneous movement needs to be considered the core of any movement curriculum, the center from which all other types of creative movement activities evolve. When we keep all this in mind, we can be sure that our movement activities are child-centered and appropriate to the needs of the group.

In the previous scene, the children created their own dance to the dripping faucet, which might have lasted all of a minute or so. By observing first and then stepping in at an appropriate time, their teacher helped them appreciate what they were doing and supported them as they added new motions to develop their dance. Later, she might build on their experience by saying, "Do you remember the sound of the dripping faucet? Can anyone make that beat again? You made some wonderful movements. Does anyone want to share a movement? Let's all move, too!" Then she might play the beat on a drum or clap it as children experiment with dripping faucet movements. To help children continue to explore new ways of moving, she could put on instrumental music and ask, "How do you feel like moving when you hear this music?"

So, as you can see, this type of spontaneous movement can arise from a sound (like the dripping water), a rhythm, a feeling, and, of course, a child's own spontaneous song. Watch your children. They are moving all the time. The interesting thing is that we don't always recognize that what children are doing is "dance." Yet their motions — small ones, big ones, hand ones, feet ones — are all essential components. And more importantly, these movements are all their own rich form. Children also may not see what they are doing as dancing, but when their movements are supported as such, they blossom even further — into expressive dancers and movers.

Once you become aware of the possibilities, you can begin to incorporate these activities into your daily program. The following are some important points to remember in facilitating this type of spontaneous creative movement.

■ *Reinforce all types of movement.* Children need to feel supported as they explore the many different ways they can move. Keep in mind that some may be reluctant to experiment because they have a preconceived idea about what "dance" is supposed to be — something specific, planned, and perhaps too difficult to even try. Ballet, rock, rap, folk, or square dancing may be the images the word "dance" brings to a young child's mind. This is a narrow definition that actually hampers a child's free expression. In the beginning, use "movement" or "move" to label what children are doing to help them remain open to myriad possibilities.

■ *When everyone is comfortable with open-ended movement, introduce the word "dance."* You might say, "Luiz, your movements are making your own dance. Marta has different ones, and Pema's are different, too. Look at all the different ways we can move! Who can think of another way we can dance to this beat?" Also use the term "dance" to describe what children are doing, not as an expectation for children to fulfill. This way you support individual growth and creativity while you help children understand that they do not need to copy each other's movements or be concerned about "getting it right."

■ *Ask open-ended questions.* The teacher observing near the sink in the first example might also have said, "Let's turn the faucet on a little more. How will you move now?" Children could then listen to the faster sound of the drips and modify their movements. Next, she might have asked, "How would you move if the faucet was turned on all the way?" Even though the questions came from the teacher, they were never directions on how to move, but ideas from which children could create.

Open-ended questions such as, "Can you make your body move to your song? What part of your body wants to move to this beat? What kind of motion would you like to add to the music?" can inspire children to add movements to their own spontaneous songs. Just remember that although open-ended questions can be appropriate, it's important not to ask too many, and not to lead children into a particular type of movement. Again, the source should always be the child. You are the facilitator.

■ *Invite children to make up their own movements.* Showing children how an elephant moves or demonstrating how to walk like a duck limits creative ideas. In other words, let children show you! And even if their movements are not necessarily what you would do, they are still *their* movements and that makes them special. When children feel they are in a safe environment, they're more able to be creative and take movement risks.

GETTING STARTED

To invite children to move in their own ways, you might put on some music and say, "Let's see how this music makes us feel." Children may, after a while, like to try motions using their whole bodies, their legs, heads, fingers, etc. To encourage them, you might ask, "How could you move to this music with just your arms? Let's try it!"

With or without music, invite children to try moving in different ways. Explore ways to move fast or slow, high or low, up and down, sideways, even backward. You might ask, "How many ways can you move backward? Let's try." Then, in a short while, say, "Let's try some other ways!" The key is: Give children time. The longer they have to experiment, the greater the variety of movements they will create. As you notice them moving in unusual and interesting ways, comment encouragingly but without too much praise (so that no one feels pressured to copy, but everyone begins to understand that you support a diversity of movement).

PROPS TO USE FOR CREATIVE MOVEMENT

By interacting with props, children become increasingly aware of how their own bodies move through space. In a sense, creative movement props present children with problems they can solve using their bodies: How can I make this object move? How am I going to use it as I move?

Props may also help a child who feels shy become ready to participate. For many people, moving a balloon or a few streamers feels less threatening than moving just their own bodies. By responding to the prop's movements, suddenly you're moving, too!

Seek out props of different sizes and weights for your collection. Also look for a variety of items to hold or carry, as well as items to wear. Remember that children's early experiences with props need to be unguided. Later, you can ask open-ended questions to extend their movements.

The following are a few suggestions to get you started.

PROPS

▼ long, sheer scarves
▼ balloons of different sizes and shapes (for safety reasons, two-year-olds are too young to move with balloons)
▼ sheets
▼ crepe-paper streamers
▼ paper doilies
▼ paper fans and flowers
▼ hoops
▼ nature items such as feathers, leaves, long grasses, and dandelion-head seeds
▼ hats and caps
▼ wings made of wire and cellophane

CHOOSING GOOD MOVEMENT MUSIC

Instrumental music is the best choice for inspiring movement. Try visiting a local record shop. Ask to listen to different types of instrumental music, then choose selections that evoke a mood and make you want to move.

Use music from a variety of cultures and traditions. To include the cultures represented in your group, ask children to bring recordings from home, or seek out collections of ethnic music in stores and catalogs.

Here are a few suggestions.

CLASSICAL

▼ *Pictures at an Exhibition* and *Night on Bald Mountain* by Modest Maussorgsky
▼ *The Nutcracker Suite* by Piotr Ilyich Tchaikovsky
▼ *The Classical Child: Volumes One and Two* (Metro Music)
▼ *The French Album* (CBS Masterworks) Short selections — good for younger children.

JAZZ AND NEW AGE

▼ *Between the Worlds* by Patrick O'Hearn (Private Music)
▼ *Chameleon Days* by Yanni (Private Music)
▼ *Nightnoise* by Billy Oskay and Michael O'Domhnaill (Windham Hill)
▼ *Winter Into Spring* by George Winston (Windham Hill)
▼ *White Winds* by Andreas Vollenweider (CBS)

PERCUSSION FROM AROUND THE WORLD

▼ *Planet Drum* by Mickey Hart (Rykodisc)

You might also look for any music by Chuck Mangione, Scott Joplin, George Benson, Dave Grusin, or Pat Metheny.

Try a Game

To help children become aware of other movement possibilities, try the Body Sounds game. In this activity, children see how many different ways they can make sounds with their hands, feet, fingers, legs, arms, etc. Choose one body part at a time, and ask children to make as many motions and sounds with it as they can. Then ask them to share their favorite one. This activity gives children an opportunity to experience a broad range of movement and sounds that they may use later with their spontaneous music.

Explore Different Ways to Get From One Place to Another

Encourage children to create their own ways to walk, crawl, and even move across the room without their feet! They may also enjoy the challenge of moving with a partner — getting from one place to another as a team creates new movements to try! During transition times, ask children to create new ways to leave the circle or to move to snack.

Take Your Cues From Your Kids

To have an enriching, creative movement program in your setting, you don't need a list of detailed, planned movement games or activities. Just take your cues from the children. For instance, if they show an interest in the clouds outside, use this as a beginning point for a movement session. Through open-ended questions, invite them to explore all the different ways clouds move. Ask, "If you were a cloud, how would your body be shaped?" With different types of music, encourage them to be high clouds, low clouds, clouds on a windy day, storm clouds, and clouds on a quiet day. Just be careful not to show or tell children how you think these clouds would move. They will be sure to copy you and then the movement will not be their own.

It can't be said enough: When children feel free to create, all sorts of won- derful things happen. In one session, children were moving like storm clouds, and another child started moving in jagged patterns saying, "Look, I'm the lightening!" This idea sparked a few more children to join in. One child found he could stamp his feet to make thunder. Soon, a full-fledged storm was underway — created totally by children.

GETTING ORGANIZED

It's true that a certain amount of noise and commotion is necessary when children express themselves freely, yet no one has to get out of control to have a good experience. You can facilitate movement without "wildness." The way you organize movement events helps create an exciting, positive, and stable environment for activities.

To set up your time together so children can participate freely and end their activities calmly and positively:

■ *Define the space.* Use an area with plenty of unobstructed room, but not too much space. A room that is crowded with many pieces of furniture can cause problems because children will naturally bump into things. Too large a space is an invitation to run and can distract children from focusing on their own movements.

■ *Hold a group discussion.* Explain the boundaries of the area where children can move. Together, walk around the perimeter so they can see and feel where their space to move extends.

■ *Help children find "personal spaces."* To help everyone find a place where they can move without bumping into anyone else, invite each child to hold out his or her arms "like a half-opened umbrella" and turn around slowly. Explain that if they are not touching anyone else, they have made a personal movement space!

■ *Take a moment for children to find the quiet place inside themselves.* Speaking in a very soft voice, encourage children to slowly breathe in the quiet of the room. (You do it, too.) Explain that deep inside where their quiet comes from is a "place" to remember to go back to when they are finished moving. (This helps children tune in to the place where their movement comes from, too.)

■ *Teach children how to freeze when the music or drum stops.* Having a method to "stop the action" is an important way to keep things under control. Here are a few fun ways to get children's attention: Together, decide on a special signal, wave a "magic" wand, lower the volume of the music, or say "freeze" to indicate that children need to pause. Most children love to practice "freezing" before movement sessions. In fact, the stopping and starting (being "freezing" sculptures) can become an activity itself. This technique gives you the ability to stop the action at any time. Just remember to use it sparingly. Sometimes, what may look like children getting wild may be the emergence of incredible creativity!

■ *Each time you stop the music and start it again, ask children to listen for new sounds and feelings and then move again.* This encourages children to experiment with other ways of moving and inspires them to think in new ways.

■ *Conclude calmly, with slower and slower movements.* Always end with a "cool down" session. This might be simple stretching movements or a lowering of the volume of the recording to quiet the mood. Ask children to lie (or sit, if they prefer) on the floor with their eyes closed and feel the "dance" that is still moving inside their bodies. Children are amazed to find that when they first lie still after moving, it feels like their bodies are still in motion. Encourage them to rest until the inside of their bodies stops dancing, too!

TAKE TIME FOR THE TRADITIONAL

As you know, the emphasis in a good movement approach needs to be spontaneous and open-ended. Yet, just as there are times when singing traditional songs is appropriate, there are times when more traditional movement activities fit. Interspersing these with free expression creates a balance of spontaneous and guided movement activities. But try to always keep in mind that there are ways to keep traditional activities open-ended. For instance, if a new motion is called for, ask children to supply it instead of providing it yourself. Avoid having children copy your motions. Ask children to tell you what they want to do next. When a movement game is familiar, you can still ask children to tell you how to play. Their way might even be better! Here are a few hints for making these games more open-ended and fun.

■ *All-in-one-place activities.*

Aerobics are currently popular with children and adults. Instead of using a "kiddie" aerobics record or video, help children make up their own exercises. Put on some lively music and you'll find that most children have seen enough to know what to do! Just be sure they know that they don't all have to do the same movement at the same time.

Stretching or even yoga-type movements are also excellent to do with children. First, remind children that stretching is something people do very slowly. Quiet music helps set the mood. Then, instead of doing a stretch for them to copy, ask an open-ended question such as, "How many ways can we stretch our arms? Can you stretch other ways?"

Even games like Simon Says can be done in a way that makes everyone a winner. Children can take turns being the leader and suggest movements. Other children can follow but are not "out" if they don't replicate the leader exactly. This way, children get the enjoyment of leading the group without others feeling left out.

■ *Circle-Movement Activities.* There can be great joy in holding hands in these old-fashioned circle games — perhaps it's the sense of being a part of a much larger whole that enthralls some children or the fun of sharing with friends. Whatever the reason, do include a few old standbys now and then, such as Farmer in the Dell; Blue Bird, Blue Bird; London Bridge; and the Hokey Pokey. Make these more open-ended and child-centered by asking children to make up original motions and/or verses after you have started them on the first one. Who says the Farmer has to take a wife? (Who says the farmer is a man!) One group of children invented a new version in which the farmer took a dog, a banana, and a bed (because he was tired!). In the Hokey Pokey, ask children to suggest other body parts to shake about. Or how about dancing with a stuffed toy or doll and having it "shake it all about"?

When you ask children to participate in song games that take place in a circle, remember that one of the hardest things for them to do is to get the idea of moving in a circle. Holding hands and moving, they innately head for the center of the circle (where they are facing) instead of around the edge. A helpful hint: While holding hands, tell children to turn and look at the back of the person next to them and then follow that person around the circle.

All through your movement activities, whatever they may be, always keep in mind that children are born dancers. And that it is our responsibility, as adults who care, to create environments in which everyone feels free to express their innate creativity, knowing that their way is one of the "right" ways.

MOVEMENT WITH
INFANTS & TODDLERS

INFANTS naturally express themselves through movement — communicating their excitement through waving arms or kicking legs, often reaching out just to show their interest in an object. Infants are also working continually to build strength and gain control of their muscles. When you respond to their movements, or even just model a few of your own, you help infants learn what their bodies can do.

The following are activities that can help you stimulate infants' movement skills. Most require one-to-one interaction, so be sure you try them when it's safe to focus your attention on just one child. Try these activities for very brief periods of time, and be sure to stop at the first sign of a child's displeasure.

■ **Show infants ways their bodies can move.** Gently help young ones wave their arms, clap hands, kick legs, and rock their whole bodies. After you do this a few times, most infants will try to imitate the movements by themselves.

■ **Alter your environment.** Try changing the feel of children's crawling surfaces by adding textured materials like fake fur, corduroy, and satiny cloth.

■ **Stimulate movement *and* a sense of rhythm.** Gently pat, rock, or stroke babies' skin in a steady beat.

■ **Combine movement with music.** Try bouncing a baby on

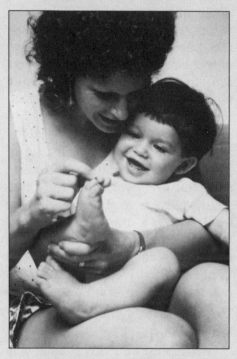

your knee while helping him or her clap hands to a rhythmic poem; or hold her by the hands and, together, do gentle deep-knee bends to music.

TODDLERS are on the move! They eagerly practice new actions, especially gross-motor skills such as running, jumping, tumbling, and climbing. To do this, toddlers require plenty of soft space that allows them to move about and explore freely.

You can enhance these efforts by offering activities that not only encourage movement, but stimulate children's senses as well. Keep in mind, though, that toddlers need many opportunities to be able to make their own decisions about how to move (within the limits of safety). Here are a few activity

ideas that you might want to repeat a few times to give everyone a chance to become comfortable enough to participate.

■ **Demonstrate new movements.** Toddlers are great imitators! Show them, for example, how you turn in circles or tap one foot in time to music. After several repetitions, many children will join in and also try their own improvisations.

■ **Encourage exploration — even barefoot!** Toddlers are just beginning to develop body awareness. By moving on a safe surface without socks and shoes, small feet can feel and respond the same way hands do.

■ **Walk in different places.** Walking up a hill or ramp, on a big sand pile, in the woods, or even on cobblestone lets children experience the feel of different types of terrain.

■ **Offer homemade "instruments."** For example, place small bells in a clear unbreakable bottle and fasten it securely, or tie a long sturdy string to several toys that make noise. These instruments add a musical element to toddlers' natural desire to shake and pull.

And don't forget, for any age group, appropriate recorded music can provide wonderful opportunities for children to delight in many kinds of individual movement explorations!

Thanks to Constance Ward for her contributions to this piece.

SETTING UP
YOUR MUSIC & MOVEMENT AREA

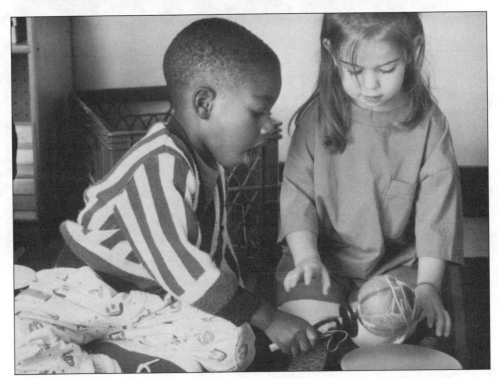

Spontaneous music and movement happen everywhere, whenever and wherever children are inspired to make music and dance. That means it's important for them to be able to find and use music and movement materials freely without having to ask an adult for assistance. After all, asking for help takes time. Children want to make their music or dance now! So where can children go when they feel like adding to their improvisations? To a "self-service" music and movement center!

A central location for music and movement supplies and activities is a place where children know they can find interesting items that they need, participate in a music activity, or listen to music and look at books. This is a place where children can experiment with rhythms and sounds — high and low, loud and soft, fast and slow — where they can play instruments or find a movement prop.

This area serves many purposes. Besides a storage location for materials, it's also a discovery place for investigations, a protected space for listening, and a place to go when spontaneous singing and dancing need a defined space to be performed.

CHOOSING THE LOCATION

Location is one of the most important factors in designing any learning-experience area, but it is particularly important for your music and movement center. It can be noisy at times — when children are experimenting with sounds and instruments — and, at times, a quiet place for listening with earphones. But more often than not, this is a place where a "beautiful noise" can be heard. Therefore, choose a location where children will not disturb others who are doing quieter activities.

Try putting the area near your dramatic-play space. These sections of your room are full of life, activity, and often noise. The real-life role-playing children engage in blends perfectly with music and movement activities because life experiences are the source of music and movement! Children will often integrate the two areas, sharing materials back and forth. As you know, it's wonderful to hear a child singing a song to a doll or using the kitchen utensils as instruments. Everything becomes a rich medium for children's creative improvisations.

Another location to consider is a place next to your circle-time rug area. It's a space that's not used as much as other places during free-play time, yet it's large enough for children to use easily for spontaneous music and movement. Because boxes of instruments and other sound makers can be distracting for children during circle time, if you choose to have the two located together, keep them separate — but with an easy way to get from one to the other when a larger space is needed.

DECORATE!

Make your music and movement area an inviting and cozy place. Provide comfortable pillows and beanbag chairs to sit on while listening to music.

Hang pictures of children and adults dancing, playing instruments, and listening to music. Look for ones that show dancers and musicians from many cultures. Most children are fascinated by the interesting, colorful costumes and the unusual instruments, and will also be inspired by them. (Just make sure that children don't get the impression that all people from the cultures you choose only dress in the costumes pictured or clothes from the past.) Be sure to change the photographs frequently so that children have constantly changing views. You *(continued on page 26)*

Photo: Kate Connell

A SUPER SETUP!

When children can help themselves to music materials and movement props, spontaneous expression flows! The illustration at right shows a music center designed for independent use. The numbers correspond to the suggestions below.

1. Make your music center inviting by providing comfortable pillows and beanbag chairs.

2. Hang a selection of rhythm instruments on a pegboard, where children can reach them independently. Draw an outline around each one to aid in cleanup.

3. Place melodic instruments such as xylophones and

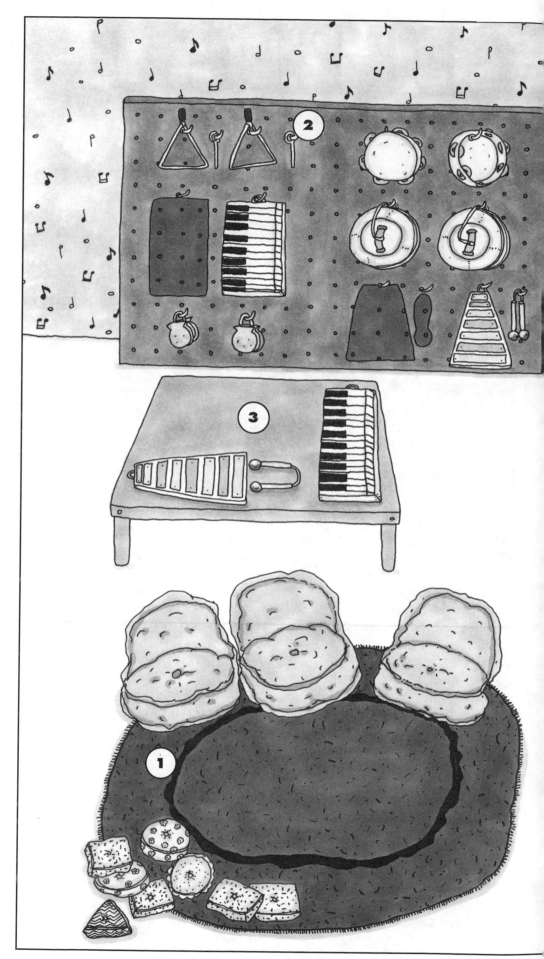

What sounds do these make?

Gadgets

4

Sound Shakers

Hats

Scarves

5

Art Materials

Streamers

8

Listen, Listen

Music Music

AIR

Read Aloud Rhymes

Movement Time

WIND

7

Tapes

6

keyboards where children can experiment.

4. Set out boxes of objects that make sounds. Household gadgets and handmade shakers can make great instruments!

5. Offer a collection of props (including *disposable* hats) to encourage children's expressive movements. Organize them into labeled boxes.

6. Be sure to include a listening center that contains music and story tapes, headphones, and a tape recorder that children can use by themselves.

7. Encourage your group to look at books while listening to music by arranging a small bookshelf near your listening center.

8. Add simple art materials for a full creative experience! In this way, you encourage children to combine drawing with music.

(continued from page 23)
can also include pictures children have drawn or photographs you've taken of one another making music and dancing.

SOUND ON!

Keep a small collection of rhythm instruments available for children to use freely. This will not be your full collection — there would be too many — but a representative sample of all your instruments. You can hang these on a pegboard and draw an outline around each one on the board. This shows children where to put them away.

Put out melodic instruments — ones that children can play a tune on, such as xylophones, small keyboards, and melody bells. For the youngest children, start with simple xylophones. Remember, they are more attuned to a five-note scale than the traditional eight-note scale. So, if possible, remove three bars or pipes to create a scale of: *do, re, mi, sol, la.* (You will be removing *fa, ti,* and the high *do.*) One of the additional advantages is that, when working with a five-note scale, all the notes blend together well and will always sound in tune, no matter which ones children hit.

Older children enjoy creating their own tunes as well as finding familiar ones on regularly tuned xylophones or keyboards. Consider providing small electronic keyboards because they offer children opportunities to freely experiment with melody. Buy ones that are well-made so they will last.

Years ago, every room had a piano for children to use, but this is less and less likely now. If you are lucky enough to have one available, place it near your music and movement area and talk together about how children can experiment on it without pounding.

INVESTIGATE

As you know, sound doesn't always come from instruments. Household gadgets, keys, spoons, and safe tools all make interesting sounds to investigate. Try setting up a small table or counter with a changing display of these items, and invite children to explore the different sounds they can make with each one. Also bring in items from home to have at the sound discovery table.

Make sound-matching games. Fill sets of juice cans with materials that will make a sound when shaken. Use materials such as sand, bells, and pebbles. Be sure to cover the containers securely with tape or self-stick paper so that none of the materials can fall out. You'll find that, left on their own, children enjoy shaking the cans and finding the ones that match.

Set out specialized sound collections. Periodically, present a collection of instruments that are similar. For example, you might have a "bell center" with many different types of bells to explore — small bells, large bells, cow bells, doorbells, sleigh bells, dinner bells, etc. Other specialized collections include different types of drums, tambourines, or clackers.

LISTEN UP!

Remember: A tape recorder is a must. Older children enjoy using headphones, so make this area easy for children to use independently by color-coding your player with red tape on the *stop* button and green on the *play* button. Also make sure everyone knows how to put in and take out tapes. Consider looking for some of the durable recorders that are being made now specifically for use by young children.

As we've said before, try to provide recordings of many different types of music for children's listening pleasure. You can also include a collection of books nearby so children can listen to music as they turn the pages.

Make a tape collection. Many children's books are now based on children's songs. Make tapes of the music so children can use the books and songs together. You might want to record your group singing so they can listen to themselves as they look at the book. Many children also delight in listening to tapes of their own spontaneous songs, so ask them if they would like to be recorded.

MOVE WITH PROPS

Provide a small collection of props children can use for expressive movement. Include scarves, streamers, disposable hats, even soft batons. Children will also head for the dramatic-play area to add costumes to their improvisations!

Offer simple art materials, too. While this area is not a place to have a full set of art supplies, do have scrap paper and crayons and/or markers available. Be sure to have a table where children can sit comfortably while they listen and draw. Perhaps Harold of the "purple crayon" was listening to music when he created his pictures!

A TIME FOR EVERYTHING

If you're concerned with the noise level this area tends to generate or whether a music center might be disruptive or distracting to the group, consider this: Because an important part of the development of the whole child is linked to spontaneous music and movement, we must have a place where children can go to find materials and to experiment. Interestingly, many teachers have found that the noise level is higher when they first introduce a music and movement area because of the excitement and newness. However, as children begin to use the area on a regular basis, the noise level subsides. As we all know, consistent quiet is not the natural mode for most young children — nor would we really want it to be.

You can always designate certain times when your music and movement area is open or closed — perhaps closing it during rest, story, and table-toys time. Remember that this is a place where children need to be able to explore.

MUSIC & MOVEMENT WITH
SPECIAL-NEEDS CHILDREN

As you know, music can help increase language skills, motor development, self-confidence, self-esteem, creativity, attention span, and social skills in all children. However, music activities can be especially enjoyable for children with special needs. The steady, vibrating beat of music is infectious, and invites everyone to participate by singing, clapping, swaying, dancing, or playing an instrument.

CHILDREN WHO NEED HELP WITH LANGUAGE DEVELOPMENT

Music is a great way to enhance speech and language development. Singing familiar songs often gives children opportunities to practice language skills that may be beyond their usual reach. For example, the sentence "I know an old lady who swallowed a fly ..." is longer than a child might use spontaneously, and includes phrases, modifiers, and speech sounds that they might hesitate to use while talking.

Songs with repetition and rhythmic beats also make it easier for children to produce difficult sounds. Children who are not able to say "bear" in a sentence often find it easier to sing the word in "The Bear Went Over the Mountain."

And singing helps children experience language as fun! This is especially valuable for children who find talking difficult and frustrating.

CHILDREN WITH MENTAL RETARDATION

Children with mental retardation often need a chance to observe for a while, sometimes whole sessions, before trying a new music or movement experience. It's helpful to repeat a new activity a few times so everyone can feel comfortable enough to join in. A child with mental retardation may also need more direct assistance than others to feel successful in a new activity. Other children may learn to blow a horn by watching someone else, then trying it; but this child might need specific instructions about how to blow air into the mouthpiece.

A child with mental retardation also needs more time to practice new skills. During free play, encourage him or her to practice using rhythm instruments, tape recorders, streamers, and other music and movement materials.

CHILDREN WITH HEARING LOSSES

Even if a child can't hear music as clearly as others do, he or she can respond to its beats and rhythms. Make sure a child with severe hearing loss can see other children responding, and encourage her to move to the beat, too. Keep in mind that children with hearing losses can often feel the vibrations from recorded music or a percussion instrument through the floor or a table, especially when made of wood.

CHILDREN WITH VISUAL DISABILITIES

Music is appealing for children with visual disabilities because it stimulates senses other than sight. Rhythm instruments offer a creative outlet for producing a variety of sounds, rhythms, and beats; and during singing times, children with visual disabilities can relax and participate with confidence.

Fingerplays that accompany songs can help children with limited vision learn to associate pictures with words, an important language skill. Because fingerplays associate words with tactile senses, they are especially valuable for children who will be learning to use braille.

Moving to music is an important way to enhance body awareness. A child with visual disabilities often has only a vague realization of what his or her body looks like, and may not understand that everyone's body basically looks the same. Giving directions such as, "*Everyone* shake your elbows!" helps the child realize that other people's bodies are similar to his.

Remember, moving freely may cause a child with visual disabilities to feel cautious and uncomfortable. But moving rhythmically to music can help him learn to relax and move smoothly. It's also important to realize that most people learn a great deal about moving by watching others. Because children with visual disabilities can't learn this way, you'll need to offer direct physical guidance to help them get started. One effective method for introducing a child to movement is to hold his hands and move them rhythmically to music. Then encourage him to move alone, without your assistance. Once the child feels comfortable moving his arms, you might invite him to stand behind you, with his hands on your hips, and move around together. Or he might like to hold hands and move to a beat with a partner.

You can help encourage independent movement by telling the child what to do at first. You might say, "Swing your hands back and forth. Now turn your body. Move slowly, like the music," and then describe what the child is doing when he moves independently. "You're tapping your feet to the music. That's fun!" Because the child can't see his own body, your verbal descriptions help him become aware of his body and its movements.

CHILDREN WITH PHYSICAL DISABILITIES

Help children with physical disabilities take an active part in all music activities. Even if someone can't do all the movements others can, he or she can discover many ways to move. For example, when the group is moving to music, a child in a wheelchair can sway her body and clap to the beat. Or, a partner might move the wheelchair around. (Always review safety rules before children push wheelchairs. These might include: "Keep the wheelchair from bumping into other children" and "Move the wheelchair slowly.")

Intersperse lively music with quiet, calming music to help children who might lose muscle control if they become overstimulated or excited. And remember that everyone in the group can benefit when you conclude movement times with a "slow down" activity, such as breathing deeply and/or listening to a soothing song.

During group times, help children with physical disabilities sit as much like other children as they are able. The most secure position for a child who needs help to sit on the floor is with legs crossed in front of the body, and back leaning against an adult who's sitting right behind her. Then if the child experiences uncontrollable muscle movements, the adult can place his or her own legs over the child's to prevent obvious leg-jerking and backward body thrusting.

Fingerplays offer good fine-motor practice for children who have difficulty with muscle control. A child might need to start out with larger movements, then work toward smaller ones. For example, instead of "crawling" fingers up her arm for "The Itsy Bitsy Spider," the child might pat the arm using her whole hand at first, then pat using all her fingers, then two fingers, and then finally learn to alternate fingers to imitate a "crawl."

If a child has trouble holding rhythm instruments, make an instrument she can use. Attach a set of bells or other noisemakers to elastic and place it around the child's wrist. (See page 16, "Making Rhythm Instruments for Children" for more information.) You can also adapt rhythm sticks so they're easier to hold by wrapping them with tape until the width is good for gripping; placing a bicycle handle grip on the stick; or cutting a slit in a small ball and slipping this over the handle. And, of course, the child can beat drums using her fist rather than a stick.

CHILDREN WITH EMOTIONAL DISABILITIES

Children with emotional disabilities may become overstimulated during music activities and consequently experience extremes in behavior. To prevent problems, divide music activities into short segments. For example, you could sing together, then move freely for a while, then sit again for another song. Loud music overstimulates many children, so set your record or tape player at a moderate volume. If a child doesn't want to participate, don't push, especially if he or she is very withdrawn. He might need time to watch and feel comfortable before gradually joining in.

You'll also want to establish clear rules before a lively music session to help children who tend to show aggressive or hyperactive behavior. For example, say, "Stay in your own space while you move to the music." You might need to further clarify what the child should do. "Don't push anyone." If you see signs of extreme behavior, slow down the pace of the activity by playing slower music and encouraging children to move slowly, too.

As you set up your area, plan to keep instruments and tape players out of sight and reach unless you want children to operate them. They are often too tempting to resist, especially for children who have difficulties with self-control.

Remember to consult and involve therapists and parents as you look for suggestions on how to adapt your program to help all of your children, especially those with special needs, enjoy and benefit from both music and movement activities.

Merle Karnes, Ed.D., is a professor of special education at the University of Illinois at Urbana-Champaign.

LEARNING & GROWING WITH

Young children are integrated learners and thinkers. Whatever they do, they do with their entire beings! Watch a group involved in creating a movement or inventing a song, and you'll see children who are totally absorbed. In the process, they utilize all areas of development — social and emotional, physical, creative, and cognitive.

As you know, music and movement are essential ingredients of a well-balanced early childhood program. In fact, music and movement activities bring together all the different areas of an early childhood curriculum and combine them into an integrated whole. What a wonderful way to learn and grow!

This four-page chart identifies some of the most important skills that influence and are influenced by music and movement. Share the chart with staff and families to enhance their understanding of the value of music and movement activities.

Each entry begins with a description of how a key skill is supported by music and movement. "Ways to Assist" helps you enhance development. "Developmental Considerations" includes reminders of what to expect from younger (twos and threes) and older (fours and fives) children. Naturally, behaviors vary at all ages, so use this chart as a guideline only.

SOCIAL & EMOTIONAL

INTERACTION SKILLS

Music and movement activities help children develop the cooperation and sharing skills they need to interact positively with others. As children work in groups — small or large, spontaneous or planned — they learn how to work together, appreciate one another's contributions, and share an object or an idea. In addition, participating in group songs or dances helps to foster a sense of group connection and community feeling.

Ways to Assist
■ Encourage, but do not force, everyone to share his or her own spontaneous music and movement expressions.
■ Provide opportunities for children to make decisions as a group — for example, which song to sing or which movement to dramatize.
■ Have an ample supply of instruments and movement props. To discourage conflicts over the most popular, put them all in a pillowcase and invite children to choose one without looking. Then ask everyone to trade frequently.

Developmental Considerations
■ Younger children are more interested in solo explorations or one-to-one musical interactions with an adult. Some will engage in parallel play, but remember that children at this age may not be ready to share materials or participate in group activities.
■ Older children enjoy social interactions more than younger children, and can lead or follow peers in creating or participating in a group musical activity. Even so, their *individual* music and movement efforts still need to be supported and encouraged.

MUSIC & MOVEMENT

DEVELOPMENT

EXPRESSING EMOTIONS

Creative expression with music and movement is one of the best outlets children have to express their feelings. They may make up a song to show excitement, frustration, or fear, or use their bodies in happy, sad, or proud ways. Through spontaneous song and dance, bottled-up emotions can be released and channeled into creative expression.

Ways to Assist
■ Support all music and movement efforts as expressions of children's deepest feelings. Expect to see a variety of emotions, not just "happy" ones.
■ Respect the privacy of children's spontaneous expressions. Observe without labeling or calling attention.
■ Be a model by expressing your own feelings through music and dance. You might say, "I'm going to skip to the playground today because I feel so good."
■ Include movement props such as soft bats, large boots, and heavy pieces of cloth to help children express anger and work out fears through movement.

Developmental Considerations
■ Twos and threes have strong emotions but are not apt to verbalize them. Therefore, opportunities to express music and movement spontaneously provide an excellent release. Be patient with very young children's need to make noise.
■ Fours and fives are more verbal about how they feel, but still may tend to hide their more complex emotions. These may surface through spontaneous chants or movement with a prop.

DEVELOPING AUTONOMY AND SELF-ESTEEM

When children exclaim, "Look what I can do!" they are expressing a sense of mastery and self-worth that is essential to development. Opportunities to create their own individual music and dance offer children times to show that they feel proud, capable, and confident.

Ways to Assist
■ Support children's music and movement efforts without turning them into performances. Children need to know that their expression is primarily for their own satisfaction.
■ Respond to all music and movement expressions with equal enthusiasm so children don't feel their efforts are being compared with those of others.
■ Play spontaneous games in which you mirror the movements a child makes, or encourage small groups to take turns following one another's movements. By following a child's lead, you help to reinforce his or her sense of mastery.

Developmental Considerations
■ Younger children feel capable when they discover a sound or a movement they can make on their own. These children are more comfortable when they feel you have no expectations about how they "perform" music and movement expressions.
■ Older children feel pride in their creations and, at the same time, seek positive feedback from adults. They are more interested in performing and often enjoy putting on a show. Although some fours and fives may be able to sing in tune or continue a rhythm, it's still important for them to express music in their own ways.

PHYSICAL DEVELOPMENT

GROSS-MOTOR SKILLS

Gross-motor skills develop through all forms of creative and expressive movement and circle games. As children explore the ways their bodies move, they practice skills that enable them to move fluidly through space. These skills include balance, coordination, and muscle acuity and strength.

Ways to Assist
■ Encourage children to experience many different types of motion, but don't prescribe how to move. Instead, allow children plenty of time to explore movement independently. Then invite them to experiment with different size, direction, and tempo movements. You might say, "Notice the movement you're making now. Can you make that movement grow very big? Shrink very small?"
■ Provide props and apparatus such as beach balls, balloons, beanbags, and balance beams to encourage children to experiment with balance.
■ Encourage movement experiences in different settings. See what it's like to move in a field, in a gym, and under a tree or parachute.

Developmental Considerations
■ Younger children need plenty of opportunities for free movement with or without music. They may tend to prefer athletic activities — climbing or jumping — to expressive movement.
■ Older children have more refined coordination and are very interested in moving to music, especially with interesting props. Their movements may be a blend of creative and athletic expressions.

LEARNING & GROWING WITH

PHYSICAL DEVELOPMENT

FINE-MOTOR SKILLS

Fingerplays, hand motions, and rhythm instruments added to singing times are excellent ways to practice small-muscle movements. These activities encourage children to exercise these muscles in an expressive manner. If children understand that there is no "right way," they can have fun and experiment freely without fear of failure.

Ways to Assist

■ Instead of showing children hand motions to a song, ask them to create their own: "Let's see. How can we sing this song with our hands?"
■ Provide an assortment of rhythm instruments that are appropriate for your group's ages. Choose mostly percussion instruments, and make sure they can be played without highly coordinated hand movements.
■ Rather than ask that children all do the same fingerplays or motions to a song, you might say, "Let's see all the different ways we can show the Eensy Weensy Spider when we sing it."

Developmental Considerations

■ Twos and threes have small hands that are just learning how to do fine movements. Simple finger games allow children to practice using their small muscles. Use instruments like wrist bells or small drums that are easy to control.
■ Fours and fives are gaining greater finger and wrist control and are capable of using more sophisticated instruments, such as rhythm sticks or triangles. Older children also enjoy creating repeating series of hand movements to do throughout a song.

COGNITIVE DEVELOPMENT

USING LANGUAGE

Music is a universal language that children use to communicate even before they can talk. Participating in both spontaneous and planned music activities helps them refine their communication skills. When children communicate through rhythm and rhyme, make up lyrics, match tunes and rhythms to words, or even memorize favorite songs, they practice skills that expand their ability to use spoken language and build a solid base for future reading and writing.

Ways to Assist

■ Invite children to create song "variations" by suggesting new words for familiar tunes. For example, the tune "A-Hunting We Will Go" could become "A-Hiking We Will Go" when you walk through a nearby park.
■ Support children's spontaneous songs by joining in or echo-singing when appropriate.
■ Introduce a wide selection of simple songs that are repetitive and humorous. Children take pride in learning lyrics and will use them as inspirations for creating their own songs.

Developmental Considerations

■ Many twos and threes enjoy singing parts of songs they know well, but may often prefer to mouth the words or just listen. Whichever way they choose, they are practicing important language skills.
■ Fours and fives are more conscious of lyrics and delight in memorizing the words to favorite songs. Many are now capable of creating their own songs and rhymes as well. Silliness and humor are very important to song making at this age.

LOGIC AND REASONING SKILLS

Music and movement activities provide children with opportunities to use thinking and problem-solving skills. In order to choose just the right instrument to create a particular sound, a child must experiment, analyze, and apply what he or she has learned. When a child experiments with movement, she learns about motion, flow, resistance, even air pressure — all important physical concepts that increase her understanding of the world.

Ways to Assist

■ Ask children to "orchestrate" songs or stories by choosing instruments or vocal sounds to represent feelings, characters, or sound effects.
■ Invite children to experiment with natural objects such as sticks, leaves, pine boughs, and rocks to make musical sounds.
■ Use movement props of different sizes and weights so children can experiment with the ways the objects react to airflow and motion.

Developmental Considerations

■ Very young children are constantly experimenting with physical laws. For example, when they try to throw a ball or twirl a stick, they learn about what it takes to make this object move. Of course, most children at this age can't yet verbalize their findings.
■ Older children tend to experiment with more refined, complex science concepts. They are more verbal about their observations and experiences, and often exclaim their discoveries to all who will listen! Fours and fives may also enjoy demonstrating what they've learned.

MUSIC & MOVEMENT

LISTENING SKILLS

So much of music and movement is based on listening — active listening to music and sounds, auditory perception, and auditory discrimination. These skills help children recognize and understand sounds in their environment. In addition, they are essential to communication and to future success in school.

Ways to Assist

■ Sing! Singing songs together can enhance auditory discrimination and perception skills, as children attempt to adjust their pitch, tempo, volume, and rhythm to the music they hear.
■ Play listening games in which children name sounds in the environment and match the sounds with objects.
■ Provide short pieces of a variety of music for pleasurable, quiet listening. Instead of asking for a response, invite children to relax and feel the music inside their bodies.

Developmental Considerations

■ Twos and threes can experiment independently with sounds for long periods of time, especially when *they* have initiated the activity. Younger children are very auditory and develop a keen sense of hearing. They may be able to distinguish differences between sounds, but are not yet able to verbalize them.
■ Four- and five-year-olds have longer attention spans and enjoy listening or moving to longer pieces of music. They have more developed auditory perception and language skills, and can often name and sometimes describe a sound.

CREATIVE THINKING

Music and movement activities are excellent ways to support young children's fertile imaginations. For example, watch as children create a dance to accompany the rain striking the roof. Activities like this are the essence of creative thinking — taking what is available in the environment and turning it into something totally new.

Ways to Assist

■ Present problem-solving situations that encourage children to experiment with sounds. You might ask, "How many different sounds can you make with a piece of paper?"
■ Be willing to experiment with environmental sounds. For example, help children tune in to traffic or nature sounds at the playground, then add your own sounds or movements. Once children become interested, allow them to take over the improvisation.
■ Offer children appropriate rhythm instruments and total creative freedom to use them.

Developmental Considerations

■ Twos and threes are naturals at creative thinking! Your job is to establish an environment in which ideas and experiments are encouraged. Be sure to use unbreakable instruments and noisemakers so they can investigate safely.
■ Many fours and fives feel less free to pursue creative explorations than do younger children. Help everyone know that your program is a safe place for this type of experimenting. You may have to make noise yourself a few times for them to realize that you mean it!

AESTHETIC APPRECIATION

All humans have a need for beauty. When children listen to music or watch a dance, they begin to develop an appreciation and define what beauty is in their world. Listening and watching activities are also times for children to relax and "be with" music and dance. It's important for them to see that while creating and producing are valuable activities, quiet appreciation is, too!

Ways to Assist

■ Invite musicians and dancers to visit your group for a performance or informal demonstration. Keep sessions short to suit children's attention spans.
■ If possible, take your group to a theater to see a shortened performance designed for children, like *The Nutcracker Suite* or *Sleeping Beauty*. Or play Pachelbel's *Canon* while reading *Grandfather Twilight* by Barbara Berger (Philomel).
■ Read well-illustrated stories while playing a recording of music. This helps children make connections between art, literature, and music.

Developmental Considerations

■ Very young children tend to prefer lively, rhythmic music that has a strong beat, and dance that is bouncy, fast-paced, and/or athletic. Colorful costumes or props can add to their enjoyment.
■ Older children tend to like a mixture of music and movement styles, and generally enjoy everything from ballet to rock music and dance. Longer attention spans make fours and fives good audiences at organized children's performances.

TALKING WITH FAMILIES
ABOUT MUSIC & MOVEMENT

For creative music and movement to be a joyful experience for young children, it's essential that you help families understand and support their spontaneous music and movement. It is also important to show family members how to recognize the value in children's daily self-made music and movement. What may seem too noisy or boisterous to some is often the core of children's experiences. When parents know the importance of children's free, expressive music making, they are more apt to support and encourage further exploration.

Remember that many adults may have had childhood music and movement experiences that were highly structured and product-oriented. To them, singing may be memorizing a song, and dancing learning steps. With your help they can broaden their definitions to include playing with sounds, movements, rhythm, melody, and lyrics.

The challenge then is to find fun ways to share the joy of spontaneous music and movement with families. Here are ideas to help:

■ *Enlighten!* Family members often do not recognize that the little songs and motions their children are doing are a beginning. Point out children's improvisations as they happen. On the playground, at arrival and pick-up times, whenever you see or hear a spontaneous event happening, call parents' attention to it. Explain the value of this type of creative expression. When they recognize these special moments, adults can

then support their children. Model how to respond to children's creativity by showing how to support and encourage without directing. You might say, "Jamal, what a great song you are making today!" or, "Oh, look at the way you are moving your whole body!"

■ *Share the joy.* Hearing or seeing music and dance created by children is delightful. So make an audio- or videotape of children's spontaneous music and movement events. Children are often pleased to be "recorded" and enjoy sharing their music with family members. Have the tapes available to check out and use at home. Take photos of children in action and post these on a parents' bulletin board.

■ *Light their spark!* Help family members find the music and movement within themselves: Hold a music and movement night! When parents have the opportunity to experience open-ended music and movement activi-

ties firsthand, they can better see how to encourage their children. Keep discussion to a minimum and play with sounds, lyrics, songs, and movement the same ways you do with children. It's fun and it gets the message across. (Hopefully this will help families see that spontaneous music and movement are more important then music and dance lessons too early in life.)

■ *Spread the words!* When children do begin to learn favorite songs, they often want to sing them for their families. Some get frustrated when they can't remember all the words. Periodically write out the words of songs that you are currently singing (both the spontaneous and traditional ones) so everyone can sing them at home. These are nice to include with an audiotape, too.

■ *Lend a hand.* Create a lending library of music recordings for families to borrow. Be sure to include many different kinds of music so that families are exposed to a multitude of sounds and rhythms. You also might want to include children's books that have a music or movement theme.

■ *Complete the circle.* You have shared the children's music and movement with their families; now ask families to share with the children. Invite family members and friends to share their own favorite music, instruments, and/or dance with your group. Everyone will feel enriched from these experiences when they are informal *and* participatory.

LEARNING THROUGH MUSIC & MOVEMENT:
A MESSAGE TO FAMILIES

Dear Family:

   As the most important people in your child's life, you can help to encourage his or her creativity. Here are ways to support self-expression through music and movement, and, at the same time, nurture self-esteem.

• **Observe, support, encourage.** Watch and listen for spontaneous expressions of music and dance. Perhaps your child may sing a song while playing with toy cars or riding in the car. Remember that a little encouragement supports children, while too much praise can make a child uncomfortable.

• **Follow your child's lead.** Let yourself join in children's song and dance. They will be delighted to see you do it their way! Sing back a line of their song or imitate a movement. This validates their abilities instead of imposing outside values and expectations.

• **Add your own song.** Sing simple spontaneous songs while you diaper, walk, clean up, or ride in the car. If your child sees you take joy in making up silly little songs, he or she will, too. Keep songs short and simple, such as "Swinging, swinging, swinging on the swing," and invite your child to join in and elaborate with you.

• **Experiment with movement.** Children often think the word "dance" means that "fancy stuff" they see in videos or on TV. Help your child understand that movement can mean experimenting with moving from one place to another in different ways — big ways, small ways, high and low ways. Or, movement can be making their own motions to music. *Avoid programmed dance or aerobic lessons, or videos that tell children how to move instead of inviting them to create their own movements.* This stifles natural creative ideas.

• **Listen together.** Help your child become aware of all the sounds that are in his or her environment. While taking a walk, listen for street and nature sounds, listen for sounds inside your home, or even ask your child to listen for sounds inside his or her own body! Together, be aware of the subtle, quiet sounds as well as the obvious ones. This ability to listen is an important skill that your child will use throughout his or her schooling. Also, listen to a variety of music together. If you like one particular style, branch out now and then and expose your child to others, borrowing from friends or the library.

• **Sing along.** Your child will probably come home with songs he or she has made up or heard in school. Sometimes these will be spontaneous songs created by children and sometimes they will be familiar. When your child sings a familiar tune, allow him or her to sing it in his or her own way. The tune or words may not be the way you remember, but this is your child's own version. Instead of correcting, join in!

   Enjoy!

                    Sincerely,

                    _____

                    Teacher

USING THE ACTIVITY PLANS

The following 40 pages offer developmentally appropriate suggestions for music and movement activities. The plans are open-ended — you provide the theme and materials and children interpret and explore them in their own ways. Combine these activities with children's spontaneous music and movement for a rich, creative environment.

GETTING THE MOST FROM THE ACTIVITY PLANS

Because each plan is designed with a specific age in mind, the set together offers help in planning music and movement experiences that are developmentally appropriate to the interests and abilities of twos, threes, fours, and fives. Of course, these ages represent a wide range of developmental levels, so you may find that you need to adapt certain plans for your particular group. To truly get the most from the plans, look at all 40 for ideas to simplify, modify, or extend.

The format is simple and easy to follow. Each plan includes most of these sections:

■ **AIM** — the value of the activity is explained through a list of the skills and concepts that the plan develops more fully.

■ **GROUP SIZE** — the suggested number of children to involve at one time. Adjust this to your own needs.

■ **MATERIALS** — basic materials and special items to gather are suggested here.

■ **IN ADVANCE** — materials to prepare or arrangements to make before introducing an activity.

■ **GETTING READY** — ways to introduce the theme to one child, a small group, or a large group of children. Open-ended questions help children think and talk about topics related to the activity.

■ **BEGIN** — suggestions for introducing materials; helping children get started; and guiding the activity in non-directive ways. Some of the plans also offer suggestions for ways to bring the activity to a close, as well as extension ideas to further enhance an experience.

■ **REMEMBER** — developmental considerations to keep in mind, an occasional safety reminder, and tips about ways to relate other skills and concepts to the activity theme.

■ **BOOKS AND RECORDS** — music selections to use, children's books related to the topic, or professional books where you can look for additional ideas.

Colleagues, aides, volunteers, and family members can all benefit from suggestions for child-centered music and movement activities. So feel free to duplicate and share each plan for educational use. Remember, when you share activity plans, you offer not only ideas, but a philosophy of learning and creativity as well.

USING THE ACTIVITY INDEX

The index on pages 78-79 lists each activity plan, along with the developmental areas and skills it enhances. Use the index to:

▼ Determine the full range of skills and concepts covered in the plans.

▼ Highlight specific skills or developmental areas a plan reinforces when talking with family members.

▼ Identify and locate an activity that reinforces a particular skill on which you want to focus.

▼ Assist in finding activities that complement your group's present interests.

ACTIVITY PLANS

FOR TWOS, THREES, FOURS, AND FIVES

MUSIC & MOVEMENT

Twos choose songs they want to sing with the help of a song chart.

SONG-CHART SINGING

Aim: Twos will choose songs they want to sing by identifying their symbols.
Group Size: Your whole group.
Materials: Poster board, markers, yardstick, and tape.

GETTING READY

Make a list for yourself of songs your group enjoys singing, then create a song chart. Using a marker, draw a line from the top to the bottom of a piece of poster board, about four inches from the left edge. Draw horizontal lines, about three inches apart, across the length of the board. (Your chart will resemble a piece of notebook paper.) Print the song titles to the right of your vertical margin and then draw a simple picture or symbol in the margin next to the title — one that twos can recognize, such as a star for "Twinkle, Twinkle, Little Star." Leave a few lines blank, to fill in future favorites. Tape the song chart to a door or wall at twos' eye level so they may see it easily and point at it.

BEGIN

During music time or as an interlude between activities, gather in front of the song chart. Explain, "This is a list of some songs we know." Read down the list, pointing to the symbols and the words as you read each title aloud. When you finish, ask, "Who would like to pick a song from the chart and say its name? Then we can all sing the song!" Allow plenty of time for children to choose — for some, this may be one of their first experiences in making choices. After you sing that song, tell children how many more songs they may choose before the group moves on to another activity.

It may take time for some children to feel comfortable enough with the chart to make choices. Consider using the chart every day for several days to help them become familiar with it. You can even make it a part of your regular routine! Try using charts for fingerplays and nursery rhymes, too.

Remember
▪ Be prepared for repetition. Twos love to sing favorites over and over again.
▪ Some twos may not be ready to verbalize their choices. If a child prefers not to speak, say the words for him or her as you encourage and acknowledge the effort made.

▪ For new song sources, invite parents and other family members to share a favorite song with you or come in one day to teach it to the group.

BOOKS
Use these books for rhyme ideas.

▪ *Richard Scarry's Simple Simon* by Richard Scarry (Western)

▪ *Mother Goose* by Gyo Fujikawa (Grosset & Dunlap)

▪ *Nursery Rhymes* by Eloise Wilkins (Random House)

MUSIC & MOVEMENT

Keep "in tune" with these musical activities.

HUM A SONG WITH ME

Aim: Children will develop listening, observation, and creative skills as they engage in various musical activities.
Group Size: Three or four children.
Materials: Enough different musical instruments for each child to have one, along with doubles of at least three.

GETTING READY

Gather your children in a circle and sing some of their favorite songs together.

BEGIN

Now ask your twos to be careful listeners because you are going to *hum* some of their favorite songs. Ask them to see if they can name the songs you are humming or even sing some of the words. After you hum a song, sing the words and invite your children to join you. Next, invite children to hum the song with you!

Another time, gather two or three different kinds of instruments. (Make sure you have at least two of each, keeping one for yourself.) Place the others in the center of the circle. Identify and play each one briefly to remind children of the sound each one makes. Now ask your twos to close their eyes and play one of the instruments you have. Ask children to listen carefully and try to identify which instrument is making the sound. Can they make a sound with the matching instrument from the circle? After you have repeated this game a few times, suggest that children take turns playing an instrument for others to guess.

Another time, place enough instruments in the center of the circle so that there is one per child. Choose an instrument for yourself and demonstrate different ways to play it — *loudly* and then *softly*; *quickly* and then *slowly*. Now let each child choose an instrument he or she wishes to play and lead an opposites game. Be sure to play along on your instrument as you lead. While children are playing, comment on their actions: "Cara, I see you are playing your triangle very quickly and it's making a pretty, loud ringing sound."

Remember

▪ Humming may be a new activity for some twos. Don't expect anyone to stay in tune or be especially accurate.

▪ Consider incorporating humming into other parts of your day. For instance, as you wash tables off for snack you might begin to hum one of your children's favorite songs, inviting them to guess, sing, or join in and hum along.

BOOKS

Here are some books and a recording to share with your children for singing fun.	▪ *Max the Music Maker* by Miriam B. Stecher and Alice Kandell (Lothrop, Lee & Shepard)	▪ *Miranda* by Tricia Tusa (Macmillan)	▪ *Tickly Toddle Songs for Very Young Children* by Hap Palmer (Educational Recording Activities)

MUSIC & MOVEMENT

Keep twos moving along with you and by themselves.

WE'RE MUSICAL MOVERS!

Aim: Children will move their bodies in a variety of ways, with a group and independently.

Group Size: Your whole group.

Materials: Record or tape player, marching and other kinds of music, and an instant camera, if possible.

GETTING READY

Gather your children together and ask them to stand so there is plenty of "stretching" room between people. Listen to the marching music and ask children to think of special marching moves, such as stretching their arms high above their heads and then clapping their hands together; swinging their arms up and down at their sides; putting their hands on their heads and jumping; and tapping their thighs with their hands. Do these movements with them, exaggerating yours and the way they fit the music.

BEGIN

Invite everyone to do special moves to the march music. Next, listen to another kind of music together and ask children to make up their own special movements to that kind of music. Try another. Arrange for an adult to take a photograph with an instant camera, if possible. After you've listened and moved to a few different kinds of music, look at your instant pictures together. If this isn't possible, do the activity again the day you get the pictures back and then look at your photographs together. Try various kinds of music on different days, capturing children's interpretations on film.

Later, place all the photographs in a clear plastic bag and put it in your cozy area with a label: "Can You Move Like Us?" Teachers and children, or children by themselves, can look at the photographs, recall the kinds of music they heard, and even try the movements all over again.

Remember

- Children may not move differently to different styles of music at first. Give them time to let their bodies hear the variety of sounds, moods, and tempos.
- Your participation is key, but so is your ability to step out of this activity so children can concentrate on the music and not on what you are doing.

BOOKS

These books will also keep your children moving.

- *Creative Movement for the Developing Child* by Clare Cherry (Fearon Publishers)

- *Group Games in Early Education* by Constance Kamii (NAEYC)

- *Music, Movement, and Mime for Children* by Vera Gray and Rachel Percival (Oxford University Press)

With bells on wrists or toes, twos will have music wherever they go!

DANCING WITH BELLS

Aim: Children will use gross-motor skills and their sense of hearing as they combine movement and music to express themselves creatively.

Group Size: Your whole group.

Materials: Bells of various sizes and types; elastic (3/4 inch to 1 inch wide and 6 inches long), a needle, and thread; and a record or tape player and recordings of various kinds of music from different cultures.

In Advance: Sew three or four bells onto each elastic strip. Bring the ends together and overlap. Sew together. Make at least one for each child in your group. Keep the bands in a basket or bowl.

GETTING READY

Ask children to sit in the middle of the floor or in a large group area. Show them the bell bands. Shake one, then put it on your wrist and wave your arm and shake your hand. Explain that children can wear these bell bands during music time. Pass around the basket and ask each child to take one (or two if you have enough). Invite children to put the bands on their wrists or even move them to their ankles if they'd like.

BEGIN

Turn on the record or tape player and encourage children to move freely to the beat of the music. Model large-muscle movements — moving your arms up and down, shaking them, clapping hands, and turning around with your arms held out. Change the type of music and continue to model movements — marching, jumping, and shaking. Be careful not to encourage or require that children imitate your movements. Help them feel free to express themselves in their own ways. Vary the volume of the music so that the bell sounds and rhythms can dominate.

Remember

- Bell bands can be used with other musical instruments. You can also add large hand-held bells for a bell music band of various sounds.
- Children might like to wear bell bands during free play, outdoor play, or dramatic play.
- Some twos may not want to wear bell bands on their wrists or ankles, but they might like to make bell music by holding the bands and shaking or banging them against their hands or legs.

BOOKS

Enjoy these books about sounds.

- *All About Sounds* by Ruth Thompson (Gareth Stevens Publishing)
- *Mr. Brown Can Moo! Can You?* by Dr. Seuss (Random House)
- *Mr. Little's Noisy Car* by Richard Fowler (Grosset & Dunlap)

MUSIC & MOVEMENT

Music can be an effective tool for relaxation.

EASY DOES IT

Aim: Children will use large muscles to move slowly and relax to music.

Group Size: Three or four children at a time or the whole group.

Materials: A record or tape player; an assortment of records or tapes of soft, relaxing music; and an open area that can accommodate the group lying down on the floor with plenty of room for movement.

GETTING READY

Take time to think about a typical day. Are there times that seem especially hectic or stressful? Do children have difficulty relaxing before naptime? Is your day so full of things to do that tension tends to run high? You might find that this doesn't happen every day, but it can occur on special days — guest days, birthday celebrations, field trip days, or days around holidays and vacations. Pinpoint these times and plan this activity accordingly. (Or use the activity on the spur of the moment when teachers and/or children just need to take a break.)

Select one or two relaxing records. Invite children to sit quietly in a circle. Explain to them that their minds and bodies have been busy all day. Now is the time to relax. Talk about how the word "relax" means to slow down, be quiet, loosen up, and feel restful.

BEGIN

Play soft, relaxing music and encourage children to sit quietly and listen. After a minute or so, model how to breathe deeply, accentuating the "in" and "out" movements. Continue breathing slowly until several children imitate you. Gradually stand and move slowly to the music. Model the movements of arms, slowly sweeping up and down and from side to side. Practice light, flowing movements, and invite children to move with you. You might bend way down and gradually drop to the floor. Be sure to use a soft, slow voice to explain what you are doing throughout the activity. On the floor, arms and legs may sweep or lift slowly.

Stretching movements are good relaxers, too. Arms reach and rest, hands open and close, and legs move slowly up and down. Finally, stop, listen to the music, and repeat deep breathing.

Remember

▪ Children have lots of energy and may have a hard time slowing down. Understand individual differences and needs, and allow children to go at their own pace.

▪ Try this activity outside, or change the environment inside by dimming the lights or hanging a sheet from the ceiling to produce a soft, billowy effect.

▪ Ask children for some other ways they might relax. Discuss how everyone — mommies, daddies, brothers, and sisters — needs to relax. [Introduce the book *Five Minutes' Peace* by Jill Murphy (Putnam Publishing Group), which tells the story of an elephant mother's attempt to relax for just five minutes. It also provides some ideas on ways to relax.]

▪ Use soft, relaxing music while children play at the water table and with play clay. This may help them relax when they engage in other activities.

RECORDS

These are recordings of soothing music.

▪ *Nocturne* by James Galway (Red Seal, RCA Ltd.)

▪ *Sea Gulls … Music for Rest and Relaxation* by Hap Palmer (Activity Records, Inc.)

▪ *We All Live Together, Vol. 4* (Youngheart Records)

MUSIC & MOVEMENT

Have fun running, and running, and running ...

LOOK AT ME GO!

Aim: Children will express their imaginations while having fun and moving outdoors.

Group Size: Two to six children at a time.

Materials: An open, soft, grassy area; and various brightly colored crepe-paper streamers.

In Advance: By yourself, look at your outdoor play area and make a mental note of landmarks such as trees, the end of a sidewalk, a large bush — anything that can serve as a marker for a running path. Make sure that there are no sharp edges or items children might run into, and that markers aren't too far apart.

GETTING READY

Choose a sunny, warm day and get ready to go outside together. As you help children with their jackets, talk about what it feels like to run, which animals move fast, and why people run. You might ask who likes to run or say something like, "Do you ever run?" "How does it feel to go fast?" "What are some things that move fast?" "When you move quickly, how does the wind feel on your face?"

BEGIN

Many young children who are in care much of the day don't get enough opportunities to run about, freely exercising and releasing energy while they play imaginatively. In this kind of activity you can provide enough structure to feel in control and, at the same time, offer toddlers much-needed gross-motor/creative play.

Take your group outside and gather together a short distance from one of the markers you noted earlier. Explain that you are going to make a path together using the streamers. Ask children to help you tie the streamers onto certain markers. Together, walk around and tie a different color streamer onto each of the markers you've chosen. Then step back and say, "Hey, let's all move over to that tree with the blue streamer. Come along with me!" Let your enthusiasm and delight set the mood of the activity as you encourage children to participate by moving with their whole bodies any way they choose. Catch your breath and call out, "Come on, let's move on to the yellow streamer."

Another time, hand out streamers for children to carry as they move. Partners can share ends and you can call out various ways to move — with leaps, twirling, taking big jumps, etc.

Remember

When doing gross-motor activities with twos:
- Half the fun is laughing and being silly together. In no way is this a race or a contest to see who can go the farthest or fastest.
- Children will vary in their abilities to move. Help everyone feel good about what they are able to do.

BOOKS

Here are some books about feet and how they move.

- *Busy Feet* by Elizabeth Watson (Standard Publishing Company)

- *Freckly Feet and Itchy Knees* by Michael Rosen (Doubleday)

- *Sounds My Feet Make* by Arlene Blanchard (Random House)

MUSIC & MOVEMENT

Dance together to the sounds and sights of nature.

FALLING RAIN DANCE

Aim: Children will observe nature and then use creative dance movements to interpret what they see and feel.

Group Size: Five or six children.

Materials: Extra children's rain gear; long pieces of material, such as colorful scarves; a record or tape player; and instrumental music.

In Advance: On a rainy but warm day, draw children's attention to the weather. Look through the window together. Ask questions such as, "What is happening outside today? What is making the puddles?" Then put on your coats, hats, and boots, grab your umbrellas, and go for a short rainy-day walk. Help children notice the rain and the wind: "Look how slowly the rain is falling to the ground. How does it feel when it touches your face?" "What do you think makes those leaves move on that bush?" Take time to watch the rain fall onto leaves, the grass, and into puddles.

GETTING READY

Once you're back inside, talk about your experience. Ask children if they can move like raindrops. Can they drip-drop into puddles? Can they drop onto leaves? How do they think a raindrop would move in the wind?

You might want to recite this poem as you move:

All the rain is falling down,
Falling, falling to the ground.
The wind goes swish right through the air,
And blows the rain 'round everywhere.

BEGIN

Put on instrumental music that changes tempo often, fast to slow and back again. Tell children you're going to pretend to be raindrops falling to the ground. Invite them to dance together, moving their bodies to the music — slowly when the music is slow, faster as the tempo picks up. When the music stops, you can all fall down into puddles! (You may need to stop the music occasionally to regroup.)

Next, give children scarves. Have fun holding the scarves and moving to the music. Try tying the scarves to children's wrists. Then continue your rain dance with added drama!

Remember

When dancing with twos:
- Dance *with* children, sharing your enthusiasm.
- Choose a variety of music.
- Refrain from telling children how to move — just set a mood and allow time to be creative.
- Clear a large area to encourage children to move around freely and safely.

BOOKS

| Share these rainy-day picture books. | ▪ *Rain* by Peter Spiers (Doubleday) | ▪ *Taste the Raindrops* by Anna Hines (Greenwillow Books) | ▪ *The Rainy Day Puddle* by Ei Nakabayashi (Random House) |

MUSIC & MOVEMENT

With a variety of music, twos will emphasize feet and fun.

FOOTLOOSE AND FANCY-FREE

Aim: Children will use a variety of gross-motor skills to move their feet and legs to many kinds of music.

Group Size: Your whole group.

Materials: Large open space to allow for freedom of movement; a record or tape player; records or cassettes in a variety of musical styles (polka, waltz, rap, disco, rock, classical, country and western, Eastern, Asian, Latin American, marching band, musical scores, etc.).

GETTING READY

Introduce this activity by discussing and trying out different ways feet and legs can move, including hopping, marching, tiptoeing, running in place, sliding (sometimes called skating), and galloping. Invite children to demonstrate different ways they can move their feet. (Some twos may point their toes, shake their legs, or sit on the floor and kick their feet above their heads.) After some experimentation, invite the children to move to music.

BEGIN

Start by saying, "Let's try moving our feet to the music!"

Play one to two minutes of each style of music, encouraging children to move their feet and legs to the sounds. Comment on their movements by describing what they are doing: "Look at Benjamin make his feet hop. Aisha's feet are moving very fast."

After experiencing several musical styles, pause to take a rest and ask children which music they liked. Try varying the volume, alternating fast and slow music, and encouraging children to change their positions from standing to lying on their backs on the floor and moving their feet in the air.

Remember

▪ Not all twos will be able to exercise all gross-motor skills. Encourage each child to do what he or she can.

▪ Arms may move as much or more than feet. (That's great because twos need movement of all kinds!)

▪ Some twos may need to stand back and watch before they feel comfortable enough to join in. Observing is as important as participating.

▪ Invite parents to bring favorite music from home. Twos will delight in hearing familiar tunes.

RECORDS

Move to music to ...

▪ *One Elephant* by Sharon, Lois, and Bram (A&M Records, Inc.)	▪ *The Polka Dot Pony* by Fred Penner (A&M Records, Inc.)	▪ *Shake Sugaree* by Taj Mahal (Music for Little People)

MUSIC & MOVEMENT

Little ones delight in this safe movement activity.

STREAMER "STICKS"

Aim: Children will distinguish between slow and fast music and move accordingly.

Group Size: Four to eight children.

Materials: One piece of construction paper for each child (8 1/2 by 11 inches), tape, and a roll of crepe paper; a record or tape player; recordings of fast and slow music from various cultures; a tape recorder; and a blank tape.

In Advance: Make streamer sticks. (Older twos will enjoy helping with this project.) Tightly roll a piece of construction paper into an 11-inch-long tube. Tape the tube at both ends and in the middle. Cut crepe paper into three-foot streamers and tape or staple a few to one end of each tube.

GETTING READY

Gather children together around the record player. Have records, a tape recorder, and a blank tape handy. Talk with children about things that move fast and/or slow — people, animals, and machines. Next, invite children to listen to short pieces of music (15 to 30 seconds) as you record them onto the blank tape. Help them listen to the tempo of each song, alternating fast and slow pieces until your tape is about five minutes long. (Remember to stop the tape recorder after each piece and leave a few seconds of quiet time between musical selections.)

BEGIN

Introduce children to the streamer sticks. Let each child choose one and experiment with moving it around a bit. Then play the tape you recorded earlier, pick up a streamer stick yourself, and move it to the music. Exaggerate your movements and sing or hum as you move the stick. Invite everyone to join in.

You might help direct children's attention to the speed of your movements by saying, "Wow, this music makes me feel like moving my stick very fast," or, "This song is so soft I want to move my stick very s-l-o-w-l-y." Call "Stop" at the pause between pieces to help children focus their attention on the next selection of music.

Remember

When moving with twos:
- Have plenty of open space available. Move furniture out

of the way, or, weather permitting, take your tape outside — the wind adds extra excitement to this activity.

- Little ones will want to move their whole bodies — that's fine!
- Because streamer sticks are made of paper (and not real sticks), they are safe. Leave them out in your music or dramatic-play area for some impromptu movement play.

RECORDS

| Try playing these records for movement activities with your two-year-olds. | ▪ *I Know the Colors in the Rainbow* by Ella Jenkins (Educational Activities, Inc.) | ▪ *Baby Face: Activities for Infants and Toddlers* by Georgiana Stewart (Kimbo) | ▪ *Sleepy Time* by Thomas Moore (Thomas Moore Records) |

MUSIC & MOVEMENT

Up, down, under, around! A parachute adds excitement!

OUTDOOR PARACHUTE FUN

Aim: Children will use gross-motor movements and listening skills.

Group Size: The whole group (including two, or preferably three, adults).

Materials: A parachute or large, flat sheet (queen-sized works best); a battery-operated tape recorder; a blank tape; a selection of instrumental music of different tempos and styles (try the ones listed below); and fabric paint (optional).

GETTING READY

Record about thirty minutes of instrumental music on tape. Be sure to alternate fast and slow tempos and leave a few seconds between selections to give children time to adjust. Also, locate a safe, roomy, grassy area (or other cushioned surface) for safe large-motor play.

BEGIN

Gather together with your parachute or sheet, tape player, and tape in an open area. Set the tape player in a safe place where children cannot reach it. Spread out the parachute and invite everyone to sit around it. (It's best if adults are strategically placed to provide guidance and control.) Ask everyone to hold onto a piece of the parachute and stand up. Remind children that they must hold on very tightly. One adult can lead the activity and say, "Let's lift the parachute *up*. Lift as high as you can!" Then, after it's up, say, "Now let's bring it *down*. Down to the ground." Repeat movements up and down using words to describe your actions. After children have had fun with this activity, put on the music and begin to coordinate your movements to the rhythm of the music. Encourage children to bend at the waist and knees when they go "down" and to reach high and jump when they go "up."

Another time, introduce new movements such as shaking the parachute. Or call out children's names and invite them to move around under the parachute as it goes up. (An adult might need to demonstrate this while holding a child's hand.) Try changing the action by saying, "Let's stop and walk in a circle." The walking can become marching or running as the tempo changes.

Remember

▪ Allow children to move and express themselves freely.

▪ When children begin to tire, lay the parachute on the ground

and invite everyone to have a few quiet moments of cloud gazing.

▪ If you use a sheet, you might use fabric paint and have a sheet painting activity a few days before or after.

▪ This activity can be done indoors. Afterward, have an indoor picnic on top of your parachute or sheet!

RECORDS			
Try these children's recordings for fun movement activities.	▪ *The Classical Child, Volume I and II* (Metro Music)	▪ *Dirt Made My Lunch* by The Banana Slugs (Music for Little People)	▪ *On the Way to Somewhere* by Kathi & Milenko and Nancy Rumbel (Music for Little People)

MUSIC & MOVEMENT

Watch children's faces beam as you musically heighten self-esteem.

OUR FAVORITE HITS!

Aim: Children will share their favorite songs, then use auditory discrimination skills to identify them.

Group Size: Your whole group.

Materials: A dual tape recorder/player, a blank tape, a recording of your favorite song, and children's favorite recordings from home. (*Note: Some children might not have access to records or tapes. Help them each sing their favorite song into a tape recorder, or choose a favorite recording from your program's collection.*)

In Advance: Send a note home asking families to help their child locate his or her favorite song. (Also ask families to let you know if they are unable to do this, so you can help work out an alternative.) Attach a schedule with each child's name and a date to bring in her recording. (You might want to send another reminder home the day before: "Tomorrow is your child's favorite-music day! Remember to send her recording!")

GETTING READY

Bring a tape or record player and your favorite song to your music area, and gather your group together. Begin a discussion about favorite songs. Play your selection and, as it plays, share something about why it is your favorite. Perhaps you like the soft, peaceful sounds, or it reminds you of a special place. Ask children, "Does anybody know a song that makes you feel special?" Sing a few if you know them.

BEGIN

Each day, spotlight a child and her favorite song. Help the child introduce and play her song at group time and even other times during the day. Record a portion of each child's song to make one continuous tape.

When everyone has had a special song day, you will have a recorded tape with a short piece of each child's favorite selection. Gather together and play the tape. Invite children to do something special when they hear "their" tune — they may want to jump up and dance, or clap their hands. Then play the tape a second time. Have fun trying to remember whose song is whose. Later, ask children to suggest names for your group recording and vote on a title.

Extend the activity with a cooperative mural. Play the tape, and offer children craft materials to express how the music makes them feel.

Remember

▪ Paying special attention to children's interests can foster self-esteem. When you play a child's favorite song, notice her reaction. (This is a good opportunity to make a few anecdotal notes to share with parents.) You might even take snapshots to display on a bulletin board.

▪ Be respectful of each child's response to individual attention. Some children may want to jump up and dance to their song; some may prefer just to smile at the special attention from you.

BOOKS

Here are some children's stories about music.

▪ *Harry's Song* by Lillian Hoban (Greenwillow Books)

▪ *Music, Music for Everyone* by Vera B. Williams (Greenwillow Books)

▪ *Petunia and the Song* by Roger Dovoisin (Alfred A. Knopf)

MUSIC & MOVEMENT

Blend music and art in this creative activity.

MUSIC SHAPES, MUSIC PATTERNS

Aim: Children "see" and "feel" shapes and patterns in music.

Group Size: Your whole group or half the group.

Materials: One large sheet of mural or shelving paper and one smaller sheet (about two feet long) for each child; crayons and/or markers and tempera paints; two low basins, soapy water, and towels; a record or tape player; and a variety of records or tapes.

GETTING READY

Sit together on the floor and listen to brief selections of music. Move your hands and arms to the music and notice the "shapes" you are creating in the air. Describe the shapes — are they big? Round? Sharp? Now suggest making the shapes on paper!

BEGIN

Place a large sheet of mural or shelving paper on the floor in an open space. Ask children to sit around the outside rim of the paper and offer everyone a few crayons or markers. Put the music on and again move your hands and arms. This time you can *see* the musical shapes you're making! When the music stops, talk about the shapes. Do they look on paper the way children imagined them in the air? Compare the shapes you made during different selections of music. Then, decide together on a title for your group mural. Hang it up at children's eye level.

For a variation, try this activity lying on your stomachs around the paper. Watch how this position changes your movements and shapes.

Foot Patterns

Put on some lively music. As you dance to it, look down at your feet. Are they moving? What kind of pattern are they making? Here's a fun way to find out.

Cover an area of your floor with newspaper and ask everyone to take off their shoes and socks. Pour tempera paint into one low basin, and fill another with soapy water. Place both basins, a stack of mural paper pieces, and a few child-sized chairs on the newspaper. Keep plenty of towels nearby.

Turn on the music again and encourage children to move to it. Now invite one child at a time to step into the paint and then directly onto one piece of mural paper. As children dance on the paper, their feet create a pattern. When they're finished, help them wash off the paint in the soapy water, then sit and dry their feet using the towels. Hang the "foot patterns" near your group mural.

Remember

▪ To avoid slipping, be sure children with wet feet stay on the newspaper. Wipe up any spills promptly.

BOOKS

Add these books about shapes to your discussion.

▪ *Listen to a Shape* by Marcia Brown (Franklin Watts)

▪ *Start to Draw* by Ann Campbell (Franklin Watts)

▪ *Circles, Triangles, and Squares* by Tana Hoban (Macmillan)

ACTIVITY PLAN
READY-TO-USE TEACHING IDEAS FOR THREES

MUSIC & MOVEMENT

Use songs to turn tough transitions into relaxing routines.

ROUTINE RHYMES

Aim: Children will become familiar with tunes sung at or just after transition times.

Group Size: Your whole group.

Materials: A few short tunes or chants committed to memory, experience-chart paper, markers, and clear self-stick paper (optional).

In Advance: Learn one simple rhyme for each transition time to help everyone settle down. Use the rhymes below or make up your own.

BEGIN

Gradually introduce children to one rhyme for each transition in your schedule. Sing or chant the rhyme together regularly for at least a week. When everyone becomes accustomed to it, sit down together and make a colorful rebus (pictures and words) poster of the song or chant. Laminate the poster with clear self-stick paper and hang it at children's eye level in the area where that activity usually takes place.

Here are some rhymes you might try:

Arrival or Group Time:
> *Tell me, tell me, tell me, do.*
> *Tell me, tell me, who are you?*
> *Let's shake hands and find out who.*
> *What, oh, what's your name?*

Snacktime:
> *Bend them, stretch them.* (two times)
> *Give a little clap.*
> *Bend them, stretch them.* (two times)
> *Put them in your lap!*
>
> *First I sit in my little chair.*
> *Now I put my hands in the air.*
> *I lower them slowly to my lap.*
> *Now I'm ready for my snack.*

Cleanup Time:
> *Tidy up, tidy up, put your toys away.*
> *Tidy up, tidy up, we're finished with our play.*
> *No more work and no more play.*
> *Every toy is put away.*
> *Ended is our happy day.*
> *Some take a nap and others just say, "Let me rest."*

Departure Time:
> *Now it's time to say goodbye*
> *to all our friends at play.*
> *Some will walk and some will ride,*
> *but we'll see them all Thursday.*

(Enter day of week you'll see the children again.)

Remember
▪ Make copies of your "Routine Rhymes" to send home for families. Attach a note explaining why they are important. You might say, "Groups of young children sometimes find it unsettling to move from one activity to another. Here are some rhymes we sing to help everyone feel comfortable."

BOOKS

These adult books offer chants and rhymes for children.	▪ *Read-Aloud Rhymes for the Very Young* selected by Jack Prelutsky (Alfred A. Knopf)	▪ *Sing a Song of Popcorn* edited by Beatrice Schenk de Regniers (Scholastic)	▪ *I Love Ladybugs* by Rach Van Allen (DLM Teaching Resources)

MUSIC & MOVEMENT

Here's a new way to express feelings — use rhythm instruments!

MUSICAL FEELINGS

Aim: Children will explore new ways to use rhythm instruments as they discuss their feelings.

Group Size: Four to six children.

Materials: A variety of rhythm instruments from various cultures, such as drums, maracas, rhythm sticks, tambourines, and triangles (at least one instrument for each child); a large box or pillowcase; and a tape recorder (optional).

GETTING READY

Set out a variety of rhythm instruments and encourage children to experiment with them independently. Then gather to talk about instruments. Invite everyone to choose one instrument and demonstrate how it sounds. Together, think of words to describe the sounds instruments make.

BEGIN

Place the rhythm instruments in a large box or pillowcase. One at a time, invite children to reach in without looking and select an instrument.

Next talk about feelings. Ask each child how he or she feels right now. What makes him feel that way? Invite children to think of sounds that express their feelings, such as loud stomping sounds for angry feelings, humming sounds for happy feelings, or quiet sounds for tired feelings. Now use your instruments to express your feelings through sound.

Together, make sounds for other feelings children name. Another time, repeat the activity and tape-record the sounds children make. Have fun matching the feeling names to the sounds.

SING A SONG

Put sounds together to create a new version of this popular song.

If You're Happy and You Know It

If you're happy and you know it,
play your instrument.
If you're happy and you know it,
play your instrument.
If you're happy and you know it,
and you really want to show it,
If you're happy and you know it,
play your instrument.

Add a new verse for each different feeling and instrument. Invite children to use the instruments to accompany their song.

Remember

▪ Threes need lots of opportunities to talk about their feelings and express them in a variety of appropriate ways.

BOOKS

Here are good books about sound and music.

▪ *Max the Music Maker* by Miriam B. Stecher and Alice S. Kandell (Lothrop, Lee & Shepard)

▪ *Listen, Listen* by Ann and Paul Rand (Harcourt Brace Jovanovich)

▪ *The Troll Music* by Anita Lobel (Harper & Row)

MUSIC & MOVEMENT

Celebrate nature with this variation of the traditional maypole dance.

DANCE AND SING FOR SPRING

Aim: Children will create and use an instrument *and* learn a new song while celebrating nature.

Group Size: The whole group.

Materials: A variety of containers with lids, such as oatmeal cartons or coffee cans (at least one for each child); an assortment of small objects that pass the choke-tube test, such as large buttons, plastic chips, or cotton balls; long colored streamers or strips of cloth (one for every two children, plus a few extra); a tall tree; and masking tape.

In Advance: On the day of your dance, tape the streamers to a tree. Try to choose a tree that has no low branches or leaves. Hang the streamers high enough so the bottoms just touch the ground.

GETTING READY

Gather together and talk about spring. How do warm spring days make you feel? Spring makes many people feel like celebrating! Introduce the "Maypole Song." Explain that you'll sing the song in your own special spring celebration.

The Maypole Song
(Tune: "In and Out the Windows")

> *Go 'round and 'round the maypole,*
> *Go 'round and 'round the maypole,*
> *Go 'round and 'round the maypole,*
> *On this sunny day.*
>
> *Now go the other way,*
> *Now go the other way,*
> *Now go the other way,*
> *On this sunny day.*

BEGIN

Set out the containers and small objects. Invite each child to make his or her own instrument by choosing a container and filling it about one quarter of the way with an assortment of objects. Help children secure the lids with masking tape. Now shake your new instruments and listen to the sounds they make. Encourage children to compare. Do the instruments sound the same or different?

Choose a warm, sunny day and go outside to the tree where you've hung the streamers. Help children divide into two groups. Encourage one group to be "music makers" by singing the maypole song and playing their instruments. As they sing and play, the other group does the spring dance. Invite each child in the second

group to hold one streamer and move around the tree in the same direction. Encourage children to move in their own ways, but remind them to hold the streamer gently and take care not to bump into anyone else. Continue moving until the streamers are wrapped around the tree. Then turn and move in the reverse direction. When the streamers are unwrapped, the dance is finished.

Encourage the groups to switch places so everyone who is interested can be a music maker and a dancer.

Remember
- This activity works best when at least two adults are involved, one for each group.
- Use this opportunity to foster respect for nature. Talk with children about treating the tree gently and not disturbing any branches or leaves. Involve everyone in cleaning up the streamers, and be sure to reuse them in other movement or art activities.

BOOKS

| Try these books to set the scene for this activity. | ■ *Hamilton Duck's Springtime Story* by Arthur Getz (Golden Press) | ■ *Over and Over* by Charlotte Zolotow (Harper & Row) | ■ *Miffy at the Playground* by Dick Bruna (Price, Stern, Sloan) |

MUSIC & MOVEMENT

How many ways can you move from one place to another? This activity helps threes find out!

WAYS TO GO

Aim: Children will explore different ways to move their bodies.

Group Size: Your whole group or half the group.

Materials: A large, open space; masking tape; and instrumental music from various cultures (optional).

In Advance: Use tape to make two long lines on the floor. The lines should be parallel to one another and as far apart as possible, but not too close to any walls. Explain that children can use the lines to show them where to begin and end their movements.

GETTING READY

Ask children to think about all the different ways that people move. Talk about some of those ways and then move on to talking about animals. How do they move? Invite interested children to demonstrate a few animal movements.

BEGIN

Begin in the position you are in — sitting! Play an instrumental selection. Invite children to sit on one line and move to the other line in any way they can while keeping their bottoms on the floor. Some might choose to slide, wiggle, or move backward. When you reach the other line, sit there. Ask children to talk about how they moved. Did they move like a particular person, an animal, or in their own way? Now go back to the other line on your bottoms, this time trying a different way.

Next, ask children to think of ways to move across the floor while lying on their tummies or backs or squatting low on their knees. Experiment for a while, then stand on your feet and try a few more ways. Help children understand that they can try all kinds of movements and don't need to move quickly.

Moving Animals

Another time, encourage children to try new movements that imitate animals and people. For example, children might move from line to line like a kangaroo, an octopus, or a firefighter. Invite everyone to take turns thinking of animals and people they can imitate.

Remember

▪ If your space is too small for everyone to move at once,

invite children to move when you call their names. Call names frequently so several children are moving at the same time.

▪ By beginning in a sitting or other "low-level" position, you help children focus their energies on creative movement rather than speed.

BOOKS

| These books have good suggestions for additional movement activities. | ▪ *Exploring My World* by Lynn Cohen (Monday Morning Books) | ▪ *One, Two, Three Games* by Jean Warren (Totline Press) | ▪ *Movement Exploration for Young Children* by Molly Sullivan (NAEYC) |

MUSIC & MOVEMENT

Move like balloons in the breeze!

THE WIND AND MY BALLOON

Aim: Children will use large-motor skills as they experiment with the effects of wind on balloons.

Group Size: Four to six children, or your whole group.

Materials: An inflated balloon and a three-foot piece of string or ribbon for each child; and a breezy day.

GETTING READY

Gather everyone together in a large room where children can move about freely and safely. (If you don't have access to a large room, move furniture to clear a spot. Just be sure there are no sharp corners or breakable objects that children might bump.) Offer each child an inflated balloon and let him or her play with it. Allow plenty of time for children to experiment and feel comfortable with their balloons.

BEGIN

Observe children's play and make comments to challenge and expand their activities. You might say, "Look at Cheryl. She taps her balloon to keep it in the air. Luke can hit his balloon with the top of his head. Let's use our bodies to bump our balloons, too." Model new movements and make fun suggestions to extend children's exploration. You might tap your balloon with your foot; throw it up in the air, turn around, and try to catch it; or pass your balloon to someone else.

Next, tie one end of three-foot pieces of string or ribbon to each child's balloon and offer to tie the other end to the children's wrists. Move outdoors and take time to note the effects of the wind on the balloons' movements. Give children time to run and move with their balloons. Try to do some of the same movements you did inside. Encourage children to compare their movements and the movements of their balloons with and without the wind. Ask, "What do you think is making your balloon move?" "How does it feel to bounce your balloon with the wind blowing?"

Remember

▪ Threes are often frightened by the sound of a balloon bursting. If possible, use extra-thick balloons and blow them up only part of the way. If a balloon bursts, react in a calm and comforting manner, and always keep extras on hand.

▪ Balloons let loose can be harmful to our environment. They often land in streams, rivers, or oceans where fish and wildlife swallow them and choke. Be careful that the balloons you use come back into your setting and are cut up and recycled for art projects.

BOOKS

The following books have some good suggestions for movement activities for three-year-olds.

▪ *The Cooperative Sports and Games Book* by Terry Orlick (Pantheon)

▪ *Exploring My World* by Lynn Cohen (Monday Morning Books)

▪ *Movement Time* by Jean Warren (Monday Morning Books)

MUSIC & MOVEMENT

Move like the wind — with a little help from scarves and sheets!

DANCE WITH THE WIND

Aim: Children will use their bodies and props as they move like the wind.

Group Size: Your whole group.

Materials: Scarves, strips of cloth or party streamers, a parachute or large sheet, a record or tape player, and instrumental music from different cultures with varying moods.

GETTING READY

Gather together to practice moving like the wind. Begin by using your hands, then explore other ways to make wind movements using arms, legs, heads, and other body parts. Finally, use your *whole* bodies to move like the wind.

BEGIN

Invite children to sit on the floor, making sure they have plenty of space around them. Pass out the streamers and encourage children to experiment with ways to use the streamers as they move.

Next, ask children to crouch down with their streamers and pretend to be the "sleeping" wind. Put on some music. When it starts, encourage children to "wake up" and begin moving like wind to the music. Notice the unique ways each child moves his or her body and streamer. Have fun with changes in the mood of the music. When it gets louder and faster, tell children that a storm is coming. How does the wind move in the storm? How do the streamers move? Listen carefully to the music to hear when the "storm" is getting worse and when it slows down to a slow, peaceful breeze. To end the activity, turn off the music and encourage the "wind" to crouch down again and go back to sleep.

Make a Giant Wind Machine

Another time, use a large sheet or parachute as a giant "wind machine." Spread out the sheet. Ask children to squat around its edge and hold it with both hands. Explain that on the signal, "One, two, three, go!" everyone will stand up and raise the sheet high. Try it, and see how the sheet fills up with air so it looks like a huge dome. Now squat down again, still holding the edge. Watch as the sheet remains in a dome shape for a while, then deflates. Now talk about what happened. What made the sheet puff up? When the sheet fell, where did the air go?

Next, stand up again and raise and lower your hands repeatedly to make "wind." Can you make a *big* wind by moving your arms quickly? A *little* wind by moving slowly? Encourage everyone to experiment with other ways to make wind.

Remember

■ Children need lots of space to move freely and safely with streamers. If a large indoor space isn't available, try this activity with smaller groups, or take it outside!

■ Help interested children take a closer look at wind and air. Put out straws, cups filled halfway with water, and heavy and light items on your science table. Encourage children to experiment and talk about what they observe. (Also see "The Wind and My Balloon," p. 54.)

BOOKS

Share these books about wind.

■ *Gilberto and the Wind* by Marie Hall Ets (Viking)

■ *Air* by David Bennett (Bantam Little Rooster)

■ *Wind* by Ron Baton (Scholastic)

MUSIC & MOVEMENT

Bring your threes to their knees with this popular game, originally from the West Indies.

HAVE A LIMBO PARTY!

Aim: Children will use gross-motor, rhythm, and problem-solving skills while learning a new game.

Group Size: Your whole group.

Materials: Experience-chart paper and a marker; bamboo poles or broom handles; pictures of children from around the world playing games; and a record or tape player and calypso, reggae, or other lively music.

GETTING READY

Talk about games children like to play. What are some games they play at home with their families? How are the games played? Record children's responses on experience-chart paper, then play a few at another time.

Talk about the fact that children all over the world like to play games and have their own favorites. If possible, show pictures of children from different places playing games. Explain that the game you're going to play started in a place called the West Indies.

BEGIN

Put on the music. To play this version of the limbo, you and another adult each hold one end of the limbo stick (bamboo stick or broom handle). Children line up on one side, then, one or two at a time, move under the stick. When they reach the other side they circle back to the end of the line and wait for their next turn. Encourage children to move quickly so waiting times are short. Invite everyone to cheer on their friends and clap their hands to the beat while they wait.

Start out holding the stick approximately at children's eye level, so they need to duck their heads a little to fit underneath. Then, after the whole group has passed under once, lower the stick slightly. Continue to lower it each time, encouraging children to think of ways to move their bodies underneath. They may try to twist sideways, lean backward, squat, or crouch. The only way children may *not* move in limbo is to crawl forward — that would be too easy! Eventually, the stick will be so low that they'll have to slide under on their tummies or backs. End the game when children can no longer fit under the limbo stick.

Remember

• Involve families! Ask people to suggest a game they enjoy at home, especially one from their own culture. If you have families from the West Indies in your group (Caribbean islands including the Bahamas, Greater Antilles, and Lesser Antilles), perhaps they'll want to join your limbo game.

• By helping children connect fun activities with their various places of origin, you help to build a foundation for appreciating differences. But remember that threes aren't ready to understand where places are located geographically.

BOOKS

Looking for more games? Try these books.

• *The Cooperative Sports and Games Book* by Terry Orlick (Pantheon)

• *Birthday Parties Around the World* by B. Rinkoff (M. Barrows Co.)

• *Games and How to Play Them* by Anne Rockwell (Harper Crowell)

**MUSIC &
MOVEMENT**

Turn a favorite song into a fun movement activity!

THE BEAR WENT OVER THE MOUNTAIN

Aim: Children will use gross-motor and language skills as they sing and play a musical game.

Group Size: Your whole group.

Materials: Props to make a big, soft "mountain," such as pillows, blankets, throw rugs, and clothing.

GETTING READY

Gather children together and introduce the song "The Bear Went Over the Mountain" (Tune: "For He's a Jolly Good Fellow").

> *The bear went over the mountain,*
> *The bear went over the mountain,*
> *The bear went over the mountain,*
> *To see what she could see.*

Sing it through a few times until everyone is familiar with the words. Have fun varying the song using different voices, such as a low, gruff voice and a high, squeaky voice.

BEGIN

Together, clear a large open space and bring out a few soft items. As you do, explain that you need to make a "mountain" in your room so you can play a new game that goes with the bear song. Show children the items you're going to use to build a mountain. Encourage them to feel the items and talk about how they are alike. Use words such as "soft," "light," and "fluffy." Invite everyone to search the room for more soft building materials.

Once you have your collection, ask children how they think they might use these items to make a great big soft mountain. Then make one together!

Now sit in a semicircle around your great mountain and sing "The Bear Went Over the Mountain." Ask if children think they can be bears and go over the mountain. How do they think a bear moves? Invite children, one at a time, to go over the mountain while others sing. Next, substitute other words for "went," such as "crawled," "climbed," "walked," or even "hopped" over the mountain. Encourage children to match their movements to the new words.

Invite everyone to suggest other things that could cross the mountain. How might they move? Some children might enjoy crossing the mountain like a baby, daddy, grandma, or uncle bear. Others might choose a different animal to be, perhaps a goat, a bumblebee, a fish, a person — anything! Think together about how these creatures might move and incorporate the movements into your game.

Remember

- Keep children involved as they wait their turn to cross the mountain. Encourage them to sing, clap their hands, and help each "bear" think of ways to move.
- By sometimes changing the pronoun "he" to "she" in children's songs, fingerplays, and stories, you help children realize that everyone is important.

BOOKS

Here are some great bear books to read at storytime.

- *Bear Hunt* by Kathleen Savage & Margaret Siewert (Prentice-Hall)

- *Baby Bear's Surprise* by Cyndy Szekeres (Western)

- *Moon Bear* by Frank Asch (Charles Scribner's Sons)

MUSIC & MOVEMENT

It's spring — dance up a storm!

WAKE THE EARTH WITH MUSIC!

Aim: Children use large-motor and creative-movement skills as they pretend to "wake up" the earth.
Group Size: Your whole group.
Materials: Blocks, rhythm sticks, and bells; and scarves and streamers (one for each child.)

GETTING READY

If possible, sit outside on the ground. Tell children a story about a group of people who lived long ago. These people believed that every spring they must dance a very special, very noisy dance — a dance to wake up the earth after its long winter's sleep. If their dance was loud enough, the small plants sleeping underground would wake up and grow tall all spring and summer. As you tell the story, modulate your voice to contrast the loud dance with the quiet, sleeping earth.

BEGIN

Invite everyone to join hands and stand in a circle. Let go of hands and encourage children to experiment with ways to move their bodies to create sounds — hop, stomp, clap, pound, and rub the earth! Gather again in a circle and place several rhythm sticks, blocks, and bells in the center. Invite three or four children at a time to select objects from the center and make as many sounds as they can, using the objects and their bodies. At the same time, encourage the other children in the circle to add their own movements and sounds. During your dance, make time for children to pass their bells and blocks to others. As they do, call and sing to the earth with this chant:

> *Wake up earth, it's a new day.*
> *Wake up earth, it's time to play.*
> *Wake up earth, you need to know*
> *It's time to wake and help things grow!*

Next, let everyone choose a scarf or streamer and stand in a circle again. Begin the chant, stomp your feet, and wave your scarves. When you have a steady beat going, wave your scarf as a sign that whoever is interested can do their own movements and sounds in the center of the circle. When everyone who is interested has had a chance in the center, quiet the dance by slowing down the beat of the chant and using a softer voice. Children will follow your lead. Slowly stop the chanting as you lower your streamer to the ground. Sit down and whisper, "Shhhhhh, listen! I hear the earth waking up!"

Remember

▪ Fours love to make noise. They also need time to just let loose. This is a great way to help children vent steam after rainy days or before rest time.
▪ Don't worry if the dance doesn't go exactly as planned. The important thing is that children enjoy moving their bodies freely.

Author's Note: This activity is based on a real dance, called the Morris dance, done by early American settlers.

BOOKS

Share the wonders of spring through these delightful books.

▪ *First Comes Spring* by Anne Rockwell (Thomas Y. Crowell)

▪ *Spring Is Here* by Jane Belk Moncure (Child's World)

▪ *The Boy Who Didn't Believe in Spring* by Lucille Clifton (E.P. Dutton)

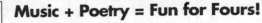

MUSIC & MOVEMENT

Music + Poetry = Fun for Fours!

RHYTHM AND RHYME

Aim: Children will practice gross-motor skills as they gain an appreciation of poetry and rhyme.

Group Size: Any size group.

Materials: Experience-chart paper; a marker; a record or tape player and instrumental music; and a children's rhyming book.

GETTING READY

Choose one of the children's poetry books listed below or one of your own and read it aloud. (You might begin with nursery rhymes or other poems with which children are familiar.) Be sure to read with feeling so children can begin to feel the *movement* and *rhythm* of the verse. As you read, move your hands, shoulders, or head to the beat of the words and encourage children to do the same.

BEGIN

Put on some instrumental music and give children time to move freely to it. Lower the volume and read the poem aloud as the music plays in the background. Encourage children to move to the music and words of the poem. When children become very familiar with the poem, suggest that they join you in reciting it, or just a few favorite lines, as they move.

Try some of these additional ideas for poetry and movement fun.

- *Rhyme play:* Some children might enjoy rhyming words themselves. Say a few rhyming words from the poem aloud. Read the poem again slowly, emphasizing the rhyming words. Invite children to do a special movement of their own when they hear words that rhyme.

- *Make a poetry chart:* Reread the poem as you write the words on a large piece of chart paper. Invite children to add drawings so they can "read" the poem themselves. Hang the chart low, where everyone can see and refer to it.

- *Record spontaneous rhymes:* Young children often create rhymes spontaneously while playing. Write a few down exactly as children say them — even if the rhymes are nonsense — and share them again at circle time.

Remember

- Fingerplays and song lyrics are also forms of poetry. Have fun incorporating many forms of lyrical verse throughout your curriculum.

BOOKS

Here are a few good poetry and rhyme books to share with four-year-olds.

- *Gorilla/Chinchilla* by Bert Kitchen (Dial Books)

- *The Dog Laughed* by Lucy Cousins (E.P. Dutton)

- *Still as a Star* by Lee Bennett Hopkins (Little, Brown)

MUSIC & MOVEMENT

Help children express their feelings creatively.

WATER YOUR FEELINGS!

Aim: Children will use fine-motor skills and share their emotions as they listen to various types of music.

Group Size: Four children.

Materials: Watercolor paint sets and brushes (if possible, one per child); thick white drawing paper; a plastic basin for water; a black marker; writing paper; a record or tape player; and instrumental music with various mood-evoking tempos, such as *Out of Silence* by Yanni (RCA Records), *Something Out of Time* by Night Noise (Windham Hill), *Planet Drum* by Mickey Hart (Rykodisc), and *Womb Sound* produced for *The Baby Pack* by Lullaby (Hereford HR2, London).

GETTING READY

Share the book *On Monday When It Rained* by Cherryl Kachenmeister (Houghton Mifflin) or another book about feelings. Go through the book slowly, stopping to discuss the emotions. Ask open-ended questions to help children consider and talk about their own emotions, such as, "How do you think the child in the book feels?" "What kinds of things make you feel this way?" "How do your face and body look when you feel like this?" "How can you tell how someone is feeling?"

BEGIN

Play one of the records suggested and invite children to listen. Encourage them to move in the ways the music makes them feel. Join in and ask children to use words to express how they are moving and feeling, such as, "This fast music makes me happy and I want to twirl around." "This slow music makes me feel tired and I want to move very slowly." "This music makes me feel excited and I want to run in circles." Play many selections so children have a variety of opportunities to express emotions and moods.

Now, gather at a table and pass out the drawing paper. Offer to help each child dip his or her entire sheet into the water for just a moment and then put it on the table. Give each child a watercolor set and brush, put on a selection of music, and suggest that children use their paints to show how they are feeling. (It's best to start with a slow, calming selection until children get used to the activity.) Have plenty of extra paper on hand so children can do more than one painting. Another time, put on a different musical selection and do the activity again!

Remember
▪ Some children might like to talk about their feelings. Once the paintings have dried, put on the same musical selection and invite children to dictate stories about their feelings. Write their words on separate sheets and attach them to the paintings.

RECORDS
More mood music …

	▪ *Sandman Express* by Chris Patella and Eileen Oddo (Musical Munchkins)	▪ *Africa Volume 1* by Machete Ensemble (Music for Little People)	▪ *Sillytime Magic* by Joanie Bartels (Discovery Music)

MUSIC & MOVEMENT

Here's a fun way to experiment with sounds.

SHAKE A SOUND

Aim: Children will develop listening skills as they create, compare, and classify sounds.

Group Size: Four or five children.

Materials: A variety of lids and containers, such as oat-meal tubs, milk cartons, coffee cans, and plastic food containers; items to make sounds, such as gravel, plastic-foam pieces, seeds, buttons, paper clips, bells, and small balls; a record or tape player; recordings of loud and soft music; and experience-chart paper and markers.

In Advance: Gather your "sound materials" such as those listed above. Place each type in a separate bowl, and set the bowls on your science or art table.

GETTING READY

Begin by inviting children to sit very quietly and close their eyes. Together, listen for sounds in your room, the building, and outside. Children might even listen to the sounds of their own bodies. Discuss which sounds are loud and which are soft. Then encourage everyone to think of other loud and soft sounds. What is the *loudest* sound children can thing of? What is the *softest*? Record their ideas on experience-chart paper.

BEGIN

Show children the different "sound materials" you set out. Encourage them to guess which ones they think will make the loudest and softest sounds when shaken in a container.

Invite each child to choose one container and one type of material. Show everyone how to place his or her material in the container, close the lid, and shake. What do you hear? Invite children to experiment with the sounds by shaking the container in different ways. Listen together and compare the sounds. Which are loud? Which are soft? Are some in between? Invite children to choose another container and material and repeat the process. They might like to choose their own sound materials from around the room. Continue your sound experiments as long as children remain interested. Then put on some music and play along!

Remember

▪ If you have a mixed-age group, supervise younger children *very* carefully. Make sure your "sound materials" pass the choke-tube test.

BOOKS

There are many wonderful books about sounds. Here are a few.

▪ *Hearing* by Maria Rius, J.M. Parramon, and J.J. Puig (Barron)

▪ *Plink, Plink, Plink* by Byron Baylor (Houghton Mifflin)

▪ *Too Much Noise* by Ann McGovern (Scholastic)

MUSIC & MOVEMENT

Build self-esteem through this music and movement activity.

THE "I CAN" CAPE

Aim: Children will exercise their bodies and increase their self-esteem as they move to music.

Group Size: Your whole group.

Materials: A piece of material approximately one yard square; non-toxic fabric glue; materials to decorate fabric, such as sequins, feathers, and ribbons; a record or tape player; and lively children's music from various cultures.

In Advance: Spread a one-yard square of material on the floor or on a table. Put out bowls with fabric decorations and tubes of glue. Encourage children to gather around to help decorate the fabric and transform it into a magnificent, magical cape.

GETTING READY

Bring the cape to group time and invite everyone to join hands in a circle. Tie the cape over your shoulders and put on some lively music. Encourage everyone to move about freely for a while. As you move to the music, make a fuss over the cape — swing it, flap it, and enjoy it! Then turn the music off and settle down for a fun game.

BEGIN

Tell children that you think this is a very special cape. In fact, as you danced with it on, you felt very strong inside —

as if you could do anything. Suggest that the next time you put the music on, whoever is wearing the cape has "the power." Start the music and offer the cape to a child.

Together, learn the words to this tune and sing it as you play this game.

I Am Capable!
(Sung to the tune of "Are You Sleeping?")

> *I am capable, I am capable,*
> *Watch me move, watch me move.*
> *I can feel my power, I can feel my power.*
> *You can, too; you can, too!*

Together, find a special place to hang your cape. Be sure it is a low hook so children can reach it independently. Then, whenever anyone feels less than "cape-able," they can choose to wear the cape for a little boost of self-confidence.

Remember
▪ As you know, early childhood is the time to build strong self-esteem. Four-year-olds need many confidence-building activities and experiences to strengthen their self-esteem and feelings of self-worth.

RESOURCES

Use these books for more great movement ideas.

▪ *A Moving Experience* by Teresa Benzwie (Zephyr Press)

▪ *Make-Believe in Movement* by Maya Doray (Kimbo)

▪ *Me and I'm Great* by S.E. Block (Burgess)

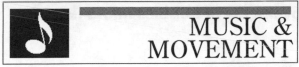

MUSIC & MOVEMENT

How can you move and stay still at the same time? Help your fours find out!

MOVING IN PLACE

Aim: Children will explore movements and increase body awareness while using fine- and large-motor skills and creative problem solving.

Group Size: Your whole group.

Materials: Masking tape, scissors, a record or tape player, and quiet instrumental music.

GETTING READY

Invite children to sit together on the floor. Talk about moving. What parts of your body can you move? What are some different ways to move them? Ask children to tell you about movements in words or show you with their bodies. Next ask, "Can you move and also stay in the same place?" Invite children to try moving while sitting in one spot. Next, try moving in one spot while standing, crouching, or lying down.

BEGIN

Offer everyone a short piece of masking tape. Help children find a spot on the floor where they can sit and move their arms without touching another child. When they've found a spot, ask them to mark it using the tape.

Tell children, "Today you're going to be doing a lot of moving while everyone stays on their taped spot." Explain that when people move, they use their muscles, and it's a good idea to start movement activities by stretching muscles out. Then do some stretching exercises together. Begin at the bottom with your feet, stretching one foot and then the other. Next stretch your legs, one at a time. Continue stretching your bodies and end by carefully stretching your neck and head.

Now stand straight on your taped spots. Put on music and move to it freely while keeping your feet on the spot. Encourage children to explore many different ways to move. You might offer suggestions, such as, "Can you move only your arms?" "What about arms and heads together?" "Can you twist your body while keeping your feet on the spot?"

After children have had time to explore, stop the music. Now sit down on the tape and repeat the activity. Ask. "What body parts can you move while sitting?" Ask children to suggest additional ways to move.

More Move-in-Place Games

Later, invite children to play Stay-in-Place Follow the Leader. In this game, the leader moves while keeping one body part in the same spot. Other children follow his or her movements. Or play a modified version of Simon Says, in which the leader calls out a position, such as, "Standing!" Other children choose movements to make while staying in that position. In both games, allow children to take turns being the leader.

Remember

▪ Keep games for preschoolers non-competitive. Children can feel like they "win" when they think of new movements or get a turn to be the leader, but no one should lose or be "out."

BOOKS

The following are good resource books for other movement activities.	▪ *Be a Frog, Be a Bird, Be a Tree: Creative Yoga for Children* by R. Carr (Doubleday)	▪ *Teachings Your Wings to Fly* by A.L. Barlin (Goodyear)	▪ *The Centering Book* by G. Hendricks (Prentice-Hall)

MUSIC & MOVEMENT

Turn the movements of bubbles into a floating dance!

BEING BUBBLES

Aim: Children will use their bodies and imaginations in a creative movement activity.

Group Size: Your whole group.

Materials: Bubble solution and several wands for blowing bubbles; a Hula Hoop, or a large piece of cardboard and scissors; a record or tape player; and fluid-sounding instrumental music, such as recordings by Windham Hill.

In Advance: If you don't have a plastic Hula Hoop, cut a very large hollow circle out of cardboard. The hole should be big enough for children to fit through easily while crouching.

GETTING READY

Talk about bubbles. What do they look like? What do you need to make them?

Set out the bubble solution and wands and take turns blowing bubbles. Together, observe and talk about the ways the bubbles move when they leave the wand. Encourage children to think of or make up words to describe how bubbles move.

BEGIN

Explain that today you are going to pretend to be bubbles by moving your bodies like the bubbles you watched. Have fun helping children "turn into" bubbles. Use the Hula Hoop or large cardboard circle as the bubble "wand," and designate an area on the floor as the "bubble solution pot." Put on music and slowly wave the "wand" next to the "pot." Invite children to crouch down and, one at a time, move through the hoop to become bubbles.

Notice how each child uses his or her body in her own unique interpretation. After a while, make comments that will inspire new movement ideas: "Can you be the biggest, fattest, roundest bubbles in the world?" "Oh, no! It's getting very windy in here! How do bubbles move in the wind?" "What happens when bubbles bump into something? Do they pop?" (You might suggest that "popped" bubbles go through the wand again to become new bubbles.)

Now use a calm, gentle voice to encourage bubble dancers to slow their movements. You could end the dance by inviting children to go backward through the hoop to turn into real children again.

SING A SONG OF BUBBLES

Add a fun song to this activity:

The Bubble Song
(Tune: "Sing a Song of Sixpence")

> *Sing a song of bubbles*
> *Floating in the air:*
> *Filled with rainbow colors*
> *Swirling here and there.*
> *Blowing lots of bubbles,*
> *I don't want to stop.*
> *What fun it is to catch one,*
> *And touch it with a POP!*

Remember

▪ For a variation, blow real bubbles and invite children to pop them as they float around the room. Or take your bubble dance outside!

RECORDS

| Here are records to use for more movement experiences. | ▪ *Music for Movement Exploration: Let Them Discover* by Karol Lee (Educational Activities, Inc.) | ▪ *Shake It to the One That You Love the Best* by Cheryl Warren Mattox (Warren Mattox Productions) | ▪ *Joy: Classical Music for Children, Popular Songs Taken From Classics* (Peter Pan Records) |

MUSIC & MOVEMENT

Here's a cooperative movement activity for fours.

MY MIRROR AND I

Aim: Children will practice creative-movement, visual- and motor-matching, and cooperation skills as they imitate each other's movements.

Group Size: Six or eight children.

Materials: Small cardboard squares (one for every two children); aluminum foil to cover the squares; glue, yarn, scissors, and a hole punch; a record or tape player; and fast and slow music (see below for suggestions).

In Advance: Make mirror tags by covering cardboard squares with aluminum foil. Glue the foil in place, then punch a hole near the top of the square. Thread a piece of yarn through the hole and tie the ends together to make a loop. (Children might enjoy helping you make these.)

GETTING READY

If possible, bring in unbreakable mirrors of different shapes and sizes. Gather your group and talk about mirrors. What are they for? What do you see when you look in them? Invite children to look at themselves in the mirrors. Encourage them to watch their reflections as they move in various ways.

BEGIN

Help children find partners for a movement game. Offer a mirror tag to one child in each pair. Explain that in this game the children wearing the tags will pretend to be "mirrors." The other children will be "movers." A mover's job is to move his or her body in various ways, while the mirror tries to copy the movements. (You might want to demonstrate this.) Suggest tasks for the movers to pantomime, such as brushing teeth, combing hair, or making silly faces. Encourage them to start out slowly so the mirrors will be able to copy. Take time to practice and have fun. Then invite children to switch roles and repeat the activity.

Next, put on music. Invite pairs of children to experiment with making and copying movements using various parts of their bodies, including arms, hands, and legs. Play music of various tempos to inspire different types of movements. You could suggest motions to try, such as swaying or twirling; but be sure to leave plenty of time for children to think of their own movements.

As they move, encourage pairs to talk together about the movements they are making. Ask them to trade roles throughout the game.

Remember

▪ Children use somewhat different skills when they play the "mover" and the "mirror." By asking them to change roles frequently, you make sure everyone practices all the skills involved.

▪ This is a great activity to do with mixed-age groups or with family members when they come for a special visit.

RECORDS			
Try these records to stimulate other types of creative movement activities.	▪ *Look at Me* by Kathleen Lecinski (Good Apple)	▪ *Family Folk Festival: A Multi-Cultural Sing-Along* (Music for Little People)	▪ *Schoolyard* by Sharon, Lois, and Bram (Elephant Records)

MUSIC & MOVEMENT

Bring this natural process to life using a fun surprise prop!

FROM CATERPILLARS TO BUTTERFLIES

Aim: Children will use large-motor and creative-movement skills as they pantomime the process of a caterpillar changing into a butterfly.

Group Size: Four children.

Materials: A record or tape player, instrumental music, a pillowcase for each child, several scarves or streamers, and pictures of caterpillars, cocoons, and butterflies.

In Advance: Cut each pillowcase opposite the side with the opening to form a tube.

GETTING READY

Talk about caterpillars and butterflies. Allow children to tell *you* all they know about the changing process. If possible, show pictures of real insects to enhance the discussion. Point out what the insects' bodies look like and how they might move.

BEGIN

Provide an open area, put on soft music, and encourage children to move around the floor like caterpillars. Tell a simple story about a caterpillar who eats and eats, then gets bigger and bigger. Invite everyone to act out the story through movement. At the end, take the music off and ask the "caterpillars" to roll up into a ball.

Next, talk about cocoons. Caterpillars spin cocoons to change into butterflies. To get out of a cocoon, the insect has to twist, wiggle, and squirm while the cocoon stretches. Introduce the "cocoon pillowcases" and invite one child to get into each case. (If children agree, cover their upper bodies and heads.) Invite them to imagine that they are baby butterflies trying to get out. Play music as children experiment with moving inside the pillowcases until they emerge. When the music stops, explain that the caterpillars "hatched" out of the cocoons. Now they are newborn butterflies — watch them fly away!

Next, put on instrumental music. Give children scarves and streamers and invite them to explore their new world as butterflies. To end the activity, turn down the music and explain that the butterflies are tired after a hard day of hatching. Encourage children to lie down slowly and curl up on the floor.

Remember

▪ Stay close by when children are inside the pillowcases in case anyone becomes tangled or frightened.

▪ Some children may try to imitate insects' movements as accurately as they can. Others may experiment with many different kinds of movements. Encourage everyone's efforts.

RESOURCES

| The following resources help illustrate this natural process. | ▪ *Bugs Don't Bug Us!* video (Bo Peep Productions) | ▪ *The Butterfly Cycle* by Oxford Scientific Films (Putnam Publishing Group) | ▪ *What Is an Insect?* by Jennifer W. Day (Golden Press) |

MUSIC & MOVEMENT

Lots of moving parts add up to one whole-group movement machine.

WE'RE DANCING MACHINES!

Aim: Children will use creative-thinking, self-expression, and cooperation skills as they participate in a group movement activity.

Group Size: Your whole group.

Materials: A record or tape player, good instrumental music from different cultures, and a few windup toys and/or simple machines such as an egg beater or a fan.

In Advance: Designate a large, safe space in which children can move. You might want to mark off the space with tape.

GETTING READY

Gather children on the floor, and introduce one of the windup toys or small machines. Talk about how children think the object moves when it is wound up or turned on. How would children move if they were wound up? If they were running out of energy? Now wind up the toy or machine. How does it move? Slow? Fast? Smooth? Jerky? Invite everyone to try to imitate the movements.

BEGIN

Show children the area they may safely use for moving. Help them find a space where they can stand without touching or bumping into another child.

Explain that when children hear you say the "magic chant" their bodies will "become" machines. Then say a nonsense rhyme, such as, "Abracadabra, pull my ear. Children disappear and machines appear!" Watch as children adjust their bodies to a machine-like stance.

Put on music and encourage children to move like machines. You might want to suggest different machines for children to try, such as windmills or jack-in-the-boxes.

Now stop the music and call out, "Freeze!" Help children find partners. Play the music again and encourage small groups to work together to make bigger two- or three-person machines. After a few minutes, stop the music and "freeze" again. Now it's time to make even *bigger* four-person machines! Continue moving and freezing until all the children are together, forming one giant moving machine.

To end the activity, put the record player on a very slow speed. Encourage your "machine" to move in slow motion, like the record player, until children are all sitting back on the floor.

Remember

▪ Be part of the fun! When you participate, your enthusiasm is catching.

▪ Watch for children who are having trouble finding partners.

BOOKS

Try these books to enhance discussions about machines and toys.

▪ *Machines* by Anne Rockwell (Macmillan)

▪ *The True Book of Toys at Work* by John Lewellen (Children's Press)

▪ *Machines* by Edward Victor (Follet)

MUSIC & MOVEMENT

Celebrate diversity as you listen to children's favorite music.

SHARING FAVORITE MUSIC FROM HOME

Aim: Children will use creative-language and music and movement skills in this cooperative sharing activity. They will also notice similarities and differences between various kinds of music.

Group Size: Your whole group.

Materials: A record and/or cassette player, a blank cassette, and a recording of your own favorite music.

In Advance: Send home a note asking families to let their children bring in some of their favorite music to share. Suggest they send in any type of music — ethnic, popular, or classical — their family enjoys. Explain that the purpose of the activity is to let children hear a wide variety of music from different families. Be sure to let them know that the records or cassettes will be handled with care and returned.

GETTING READY

At group time, talk about your favorite music. Bring in a few examples of the types of music you like to listen to. (It's a good idea to have a variety, and, if possible, share music from your cultural heritage.) Encourage children to move freely, hum, or sing along. Later, you can discuss how the music is the same or different from the music children listen to at home. Then propose a "Family Favorite Music Week."

BEGIN

Set up your week so that only a few children share their music each day. This way, there won't be too many children waiting for a turn. Invite each child to introduce his or her recording, if she'd like, and tell a little bit about when she listens to it at home.

Then play the music. At first, just sit and listen. Some children may want to clap, hum, or sing along. Many might say, "I know that music, too!"

Once children have had time to listen, invite their interpretations by saying, "This music makes me feel like moving. How about you? Let's stand up and see how this music makes us all feel." Play the selection long enough for children to experiment with their motions and their coordination.

Later, play another child's selection and repeat the process. Encourage children to make comparisons but make sure no selection is labeled "better" than another. If possible, make a cassette recording so you'll have the music to play again. These can be compiled into "Our Favorite Family Music Collection" to use for movement and listening activities throughout the year.

Remember

▪ Some children's favorite music from home may be "live" music played by a family member. If so, invite the family member to come and share his or her music with your group. Ask if you can tape the performance.

▪ Because fives are ready to begin looking at the world from a less egocentric point of view, they are able to appreciate each other's similarities and differences, as well as see themselves as part of a group. This activity helps children develop strong self-concepts and provides opportunities to share a part of their cultural heritage.

▪ Focus on cultural, classical, and popular music instead of a particular category, such as holiday music. In this way, children get to hear and respond to a wide variety of music.

BOOKS

Here are some children's books with a musical theme.

▪ *I See a Song* by Eric Carle (Thomas Y. Crowell)

▪ *Max the Music Maker* by Miriam B. Stecher and Alice S. Kandell (Lothrop, Lee & Shepard)

▪ *Something Special for Me* by Vera B. Williams (Greenwillow Books)

MUSIC & MOVEMENT

Children's play becomes music to their ears.

STRIKE UP THE GADGET BAND!

Aim: Children will use creative-thinking and expression skills to create their own instruments.

Group Size: Four or five children at a time.

Materials: A variety of objects you might find in your setting or a kitchen, such as rulers, pencils, paper clip boxes, a grater, a hand eggbeater, measuring spoons, and empty plastic bottles; a record or tape player; and recorded marching music.

GETTING READY

Put out a variety of safe-to-handle gadgets, and let children explore and play with them. Pick up on their interests and together brainstorm different ways to make sounds using the objects. Invite children to choose one, and explore the different sounds they can make. Encourage them to try many different methods and come up with ideas to make sounds, such as rattling, tapping, blowing, rubbing, etc.

BEGIN

Invite small groups of children to look around the room for additional objects to use in a gadget band. Explain that once they've found an object or two, they can use any of the sound-making methods you've already talked about. Give children plenty of time to experiment with their newfound "instruments," and demonstrate the different sounds for one another.

Organize your gadget band. Gather all the musicians together, put on some marching music, and invite the band to parade around the room. At various times, suggest that children try to vary the sounds they make with their instruments. Also, vary the volume of the music so children can try playing their instruments loudly and softly.

Here's a song you can sing together.

The Gadget Band
(Tune: "The Mulberry Bush")

> The gadget band has come to school,
> Come to school, come to school.
> The gadget band has come to school
> To play for all its friends.
> Let's all make a tapping (rattling, rubbing, etc.)
> sound,
> A tapping sound, a tapping sound.
> Let's all make a tapping sound,
> And play for all our friends.

Remember

- Because five-year-olds are naturally curious about sound, you may find that they will experiment frequently over the next few days. Extend this activity by inviting them to bring in a gadget from home to use in the band.
- Allow children to try unusual combinations of objects to create sound.
- Your band can play along with favorite songs. Ask children to choose which gadget sounds complement each other.

BOOKS

Share these music-making books.

- *Thump, Thump, Rat-a-Tat-Tat* by Gene Baer (Harper Trophy)

- *Max the Music Maker* by Miriam B. Stecher and Alice S. Kandell (Lothrop, Lee & Shepard)

- *Miranda* by Tricia Tusa (Macmillan)

ACTIVITY PLAN
READY-TO-USE TEACHING IDEAS FOR FIVES

MUSIC & MOVEMENT

Use the noises outside to create your own spontaneous music.

SPONTANEOUS SOUNDS OF THE PLAYGROUND

Aim: Children will use creative-thinking, listening, and expression skills.
Group Size: Four or five children.
Materials: Active imaginations and rhythm instruments.

GETTING READY

Prior to going outside, gather children together to choose and sing some favorite songs. If possible, encourage them to add rhythm instruments to the music. Ask them to listen to each song and choose instruments they think will add to the rhythm.

BEGIN

Later, invite children to think about the sounds they hear on the playground. You might ask, "What sounds do you think we will hear outside today? Which sounds will be loud and which will be soft?" (It's important to help children think about sounds *before* you go out.)

Once outside, invite children to go on a "sound scavenger hunt." Ask everyone to listen carefully for different types of sounds and encourage them to report back. After you've "collected" sounds, invite children to create spontaneous music.

First ask, "Can you imitate any of the sounds you heard?" Give everyone time to practice and experiment with imitating and guessing. Then say, "Let's see if we can put all the different sounds together to create our own music!" Step back and listen as children experiment with sounds. Some might want to use the different sounds to answer back the sounds they hear in the environment.

At some point, children may be ready to add another dimension to this spontaneous music play. Together, you can listen to the outdoor sounds and find instruments to complement them. With this addition, your music play may take off in many directions. You might even see children create a spontaneous marching band!

Remember

▪ Because there is so much to see and do, the playground can be a distracting place for children. Don't expect everyone to stay with this activity for a long period of time. You'll probably find that children would prefer to move in and out.
▪ This is a spontaneous music activity. Rather than direct the event, provide children with sparks to ignite their creative thinking.

BOOKS

Enhance your storytime with these books about sounds.

▪ *Listen to That* by H. Klurfmeier (Western)

▪ *Max, the Music Maker* by Miriam B. Stecher & Alice S. Kandell (Lothrop, Lee & Shepard)

▪ *The Country Noisy Book* by Margaret Wise Brown (Harper & Row)

MUSIC & MOVEMENT

Here's a new way to use the rhythm instruments in your room.

ORCHESTRATE A FAVORITE STORY

Aim: Children will use listening, music, and creative thinking skills in this activity.

Group Size: Your whole group.

Materials: Rhythm instruments from various cultures, chart paper, and a favorite *repetitive* story.

In Advance: Choose a familiar, simple story that has characters and lines that repeat (*The Three Billy Goats Gruff, The Gingerbread Man, What Do You Do With a Kangaroo?*, and *The House That Jack Built* are all good choices.) It isn't necessary to have the actual book if you can tell the tale from memory. What is most important is repeating the names of the characters frequently.

BEGIN

Read or tell the story so that it's familiar to your children. Discuss the different characters and what they do. Take note of the specific traits of the characters: *big* or *small*, *young* or *old*, *good* or *bad*, etc.

Introduce the collection of instruments and explain to children that they are going to help tell the story using the instruments. Pass out one instrument to each child and have him or her play it so the group can hear its sound. Next, name a character in the story. Talk about an obvious trait of that character. Based on the trait, help children choose an instrument to represent that character. For example, in *The Three Billy Goats Gruff*, the biggest billy goat might be represented by a drum and the littlest by a bell. You might want to make a rebus chart that shows the choices by drawing a picture of the character and, next to it, the instrument that represents it.

You can also help children choose instruments to represent sound effects in the story. For example, in *The Three Billy Goats Gruff*, wood blocks could make the sound of the goats clomping over the bridge.

Seat children with similar instruments together. Explain that when you tell the story, they will have to listen very carefully. When they hear their character's name or the action for their sound effect, it's time to play their instrument.

Now read or retell the story, pausing as you name characters and sounds to give children time to play. Repeat just for fun and practice, and then give children an opportunity to play other instruments.

This same process can be used with a repetitive song such as "The Wheels on the Bus," "I Know an Old Lady," or "Old MacDonald." Help children choose instruments to represent things, animals, or people. As they sing, help them listen for their sound or animal and play their instrument when they hear their cue.

Remember

▪ Though this activity may seem teacher-directed, if you leave the instruments out, you'll find that children will begin to develop their own sound stories by themselves.

▪ Sometimes children will have a different idea than you of what instrument to pair with a particular character. If that happens, simply go with their suggestions.

BOOKS

Here are some good books you might use.

▪ *The Three Billy Goats Gruff* by Peter Christian Asbjornsen (Harcourt Brace Jovanovich)

▪ *Stone Soup* by Marcia Brown (Scholastic)

▪ *The House That Jack Built* by Paul Galdone (McGraw-Hill)

MUSIC & MOVEMENT

Most five-year-olds delight in discovering this new way to make sounds!

LET'S HAVE A KAZOO PARADE!

Aim: Children will use creative-thinking, fine-motor, gross-motor, listening, and speaking skills.

Group Size: Two or three at a time during construction and your whole group for the parade.

Materials: Cardboard toilet paper or paper towel tubes cut in half, waxed paper, rubber bands, non-toxic markers and crayons, a pen or pencil, rhythm instruments, a record or tape player, and a good marching record or tape.

GETTING READY

Put on some marching music and invite children to choose an instrument and join in the band. Periodically, stop the group and encourage just the drummers to march and make their sounds. Then ask another instrument to play alone. This way every child gets to march with both a large group and a small one. It also helps children hear the sounds that each instrument makes.

BEGIN

Gather a few children together at a table to make kazoos. Show them the tubes and ask them how they think they could use them to make a sound. Some children will immediately blow into it like a horn, while others will tap it like a drumstick. Say, "I have an easy way to make an instrument called a kazoo. We can make them together."

Pass out crayons and markers and invite children to decorate the outside of their tubes. When they're finished, help each child use a pencil or pen to make a hole in the side of the tube about two-thirds of the way down. Then help them hold a piece of waxed paper over the end of the tube as you secure it with a rubber band. Now your kazoos are finished and ready for action.

Together, hum an easy favorite song such as "Row, Row, Row Your Boat." Show children how to hum into the open end of the kazoo. Some may try to blow at first, but will soon see that it doesn't work that way. Eventually, your whole group will be humming along!

March around the room and/or school a few times, then right out the door, around the playground, and back to the play area to sit down for a rest! Kazoo-playing takes a lot of wind!

Remember

▪ The trick to playing a kazoo is in the humming. Remind children that when you hum you keep your mouth closed and your lips together.

▪ When you march together, you can choose a song to hum, but most children will be more interested in humming their own tune.

BOOKS

Share these music-making books.

▪ *I See a Song* by Eric Carle (Thomas Y. Crowell)

▪ *Music, Music for Everyone* by Vera B. Williams (Greenwillow Books)

▪ *The Troll Music* by Anita Lobel (Harper & Row)

MUSIC & MOVEMENT

Encourage children to get involved with one another.

COME-AND-GO PARTNERS

Aim: Children will use problem-solving and cooperation skills as well as creative-movement ideas.
Group Size: Your whole group.
Materials: A record or tape player, and the lively music of artists such as Sweet Honey in the Rock, Dave Grusin, Pat Metheny, and Spirogyra.

GETTING READY

Before you begin, explain to children that they will be participating in activities that are cooperative — in which everyone wins and everyone helps each other. If possible, read one of the books listed below to reinforce the idea of partners helping each other.

BEGIN

To start, try this fun way to pick partners. Ask half of the group to form a circle. Then ask the other half to make a circle around them. Put on some music and ask children to walk around in their circles in opposite directions. When the music stops, ask the people in the center circle to turn and face the outer circle. Whomever they are facing is their partner!

Put on some music so children can move. Explain that partners can do whatever movements they would like but they need to try to do the same thing together. Every so often, call out movement questions. "Can you and your partner move in *very small* ways? *Very big* ways? Can you move backward together? Make spinning motions together?" Allow enough time between suggestions for children to really problem-solve about how they are going to do their movements together. This is one way for children to learn and practice thinking cooperatively.

Another time, ask children to stand with their partners while they wait for the music to start. Explain that as soon as the music begins, they can move any way they'd like *away* from their partners. When the music stops, they will need to find their partners and sit down together. Play this sequence at least a few times. (Most probably, you'll notice that children will delight in this simple game because of the fun of trying to find their partners again. Most will giggle as they watch their partner from afar and rejoice in coming back together. Watch the fun as you vary the amount of time between the starting and stopping.)

Remember

- Choosing partners can be difficult for some children. This is one reason why this is an important cooperative activity. You might need to volunteer to be a child's partner to get him or her started. Once children are warmed up, they usually become accustomed to the idea of partners. If possible, invite children to change partners using the partner-choosing game.
- Some children are uncomfortable holding a partner's hand. Let them know they have the option of standing or sitting next to each other without touching.
- Encourage children to use all different types of movements such as sliding, crawling, sidestepping, and twirling.

BOOKS

| Here are books in which partners work and play together. | ▪ *Frog and Toad Are Friends* by Arnold Lobel (Scholastic) | ▪ *Frog and Toad Together* by Arnold Lobel (Scholastic) | ▪ *George and Martha* by James Marshall (Houghton Mifflin) |

MUSIC & MOVEMENT

Celebrate the fall with this expressive-movement activity.

THE DANCE OF THE FALLING LEAVES

Aim: Children will use creative and expressive movement, as well as gross-motor skills.

Group Size: Your whole group

Materials: A record or tape player; recorded instrumental movement music, such as "Caverna Magica" by Andreas Vollenweider or "Silk Road" by Kitaro; streamers or scarves and balloons in fall colors (yellow, red, orange, brown, etc.); and brooms.

GETTING READY

If possible, sit with children outside on a windy fall day and watch the leaves fall and dance. (If you live in an area where you don't have fall leaves, share the books listed below and talk about the autumn season and the beautiful fall colors.) Talk about the way leaves fall, asking, "Do you think leaves fall fast or slow? How do you think they move?" Invite children to use their hands and arms to imitate the motions of the leaves.

Encourage children to observe the leaves that haven't fallen yet, and help children describe how they move when they're still on the tree. Together, flutter like the leaves on the tree and watch to see if any real leaves get caught in the wind. How do they move up and down on their way to the ground?

Stand up and move, encouraging everyone to do their own "dance of the leaves." Incorporate children's delight in chasing the leaves and trying to catch them.

BEGIN

Back inside, gather everyone in a circle on the floor. Play selections and ask children to listen for music that sounds good for dancing leaves. Encourage everyone to choose a streamer or scarf and practice moving their streamers in the same ways leaves move — up and down, spinning, and swaying from side to side.

Then say, "Let's pretend we're leaves on a tree. When the wind blows, we'll start to wiggle and move, and eventually fall off our tree and dance through the air." Put on the music and stand in the middle of the group with your arms outstretched as if you were a tree. Invite everyone to be "leaves" or "trees." Start making sounds like the wind and move to the music. As the wind blows harder, suggest that the "leaves" fall off the "tree" and float around the room swirling their streamers. As the music comes to a close, start turning down

the volume. Explain that the wind has slowed down now, so it's time for the leaves to gently land on the ground.

Try the Dance With Balloons!

On another day, try the dance of the falling leaves with fall-colored balloons instead of streamers or scarves. Children can enjoy trying to keep the balloon "leaves" up in the air by gently tapping them with different parts of their bodies. Remind everyone that most leaves seem to fall slowly and gently, so it's important to touch the balloons gently. End the dance by letting all of the balloons fall to the floor. Invite a few children to use a broom to "rake" the balloon "leaves" into a pile.

Remember

▪ Encourage "your leaves" to fall and move any way they want. Your goal is to inspire individual interpretations.

▪ Balloons can be hazardous to the environment. When you are through with the activity, let the balloons deflate, cut them up, and use the pieces as scraps for art collages.

BOOKS

Include these books in your fall celebration!	▪ *All Falling Down* by Gene Zion (Harper & Row)	▪ *The Wonderful Tree* by Adelaide Holl (Golden Press)	▪ *Down Come the Leaves* by Henrietta Bancroft (Thomas Y. Crowell)

MUSIC & MOVEMENT

"Magic" wands help children move to the beat of special drummers — themselves!

MAGIC DANCING

Aim: Children will use large-motor and creative-movement skills as they experiment with dancing to various tempos.
Group Size: Your whole group.
Materials: Paper towel tubes (one for each child), ribbons, multicolored tissue paper, glue, a stapler, a shallow container, a record or tape player, and instrumental music of different cultures that changes tempos and moods.

GETTING READY

Help children tear tissue paper into small squares, approximately one inch wide. Mix white craft glue with water (in equal measures) and put the mixture out in shallow containers. Invite children to help you cover a table with newspaper and then put on smocks. Offer each child a paper towel tube and show him or her how to dip a tissue-paper square carefully into the watered-down glue and place the square on the paper tube. It will stick! (Note: Tissue paper colors will run and overlap. If children are concerned, explain that this is part of the design.) Let the tubes dry overnight. The next day, help children staple colorful ribbons to one end of their tubes, and Presto! You have magic wands!

BEGIN

Bring children together and invite them to share what they would do with a magic wand. Then clear an open space where children can move about freely. Join hands in a large circle, with two or three children in the middle. Ask everyone in the outside circle to call out ways for the children in the middle to move. They might suggest *jumpy*, *smooth*, *fast*, *silly*, *heavy*, *sleepy*, etc.

Now, pass out all the magic wands and put on the music. Say, "Let your magic wand move you the way the music makes you feel." Join the children as they take turns moving and watching, using exaggerated movements with your body and wand. As the record plays and tempos change, invite children to match their movements to the new sounds, saying, "Listen to the music. It is moving very slowly. How can your magic wand move your body to this music?"

Eventually, most children will be up and moving. If their interest continues, invite one child to be the "conductor" and stand where everyone can see him. Ask that child

to use just his wand to show the movements of the music. Each time the music changes and there is a new movement, ask the child to call out, "Change!" Encourage the other children to watch the conductor. Take turns, and then end with a very slow, sleepy selection.

Remember
▪ Your voice and mannerisms can bring magic to this activity and help children become truly involved.

BOOKS

Here are special magical stories to add to the fantasy of this activity.

▪ *Magical Changes* by Graham Oakley (Viking)

▪ *Sylvester and the Magic Pebble* by William Steig (Simon & Schuster)

▪ *Watch Out! A Giant!* by Eric Carle (Collins)

MUSIC & MOVEMENT

Create moving sculptures with your five-year-olds.

MOVEMENT SCULPTURES

Aim: Children will use their bodies to create sculptures to music.
Group Size: Four to six children.
Materials: A large bed sheet; a record or tape player; recorded music that suggests different moods; and, for enrichment, *Norman the Doorman* by Don Freeman (Penguin).

GETTING READY

Talk to children about sculptures. What do they think a sculpture is? Where have they seen sculptures before? At a museum, or in the park? If possible, bring in a few small sculptures or pictures to illustrate your discussion. Also read *Norman the Doorman*, a story about a little mouse who lives in a museum, makes a sculpture out of junk material, and wins first prize in a contest.

BEGIN

Explain to children that they can become sculptures with the help of some friends, some music, and a sheet. Then ask about six children to go under the sheet with you. While the music is playing, move, twist, shake, and curl the sheet. When the music stops everyone will need to freeze — into a sculpture. Ask the other children to watch and describe the sculptures as they form.

Encourage children to try many positions and repeat the activity several times so everyone gets many turns. Each time a new group starts, try giving them a theme along with new music — animals, machines, houses, and, of course, terrific ghost sculptures!

Remember

▪ Some children may prefer to watch a couple of times before they feel comfortable going under the sheet. Let them choose to remain outside as long as they'd like without drawing attention to their preference.

BOOKS

Here are some books on sculptures and museums.	▪ *Faces on Places* by Suzanne Haldane (Viking)	▪ *I Carve Stone* by Joan Fine (Thomas Y. Crowell)	▪ *When Clay Sings* by Byrd Baylor (Charles Scribner's Sons)

MUSIC & MOVEMENT

Imaginations will soar as children take a fantasy trip inside a magical pumpkin!

A MAGIC PUMPKIN JOURNEY

Aim: Children will use creative expression and their imaginations while participating in a guided fantasy.

Group Size: Your whole group.

Materials: Edible pumpkin seeds, small inflated balloons hidden inside a large pillowcase or plastic bag, a record or tape player, and gentle music from various cultures.

GETTING READY

Talk about the word "journey." Ask, "What is a journey?" "How do people take journeys?" "Are journeys always real or are they sometimes pretend?"

Explain that today you are going to let your imaginations take a *pretend* journey inside a magic pumpkin. Ask, "What do you think we would see if we were inside a pumpkin?" "Could we go inside a *real* pumpkin?"

BEGIN

Organize your children in a circle sitting on the floor, and place the bag of balloons in the center. Discuss your journey. "How big would the pumpkin have to be to fit all of us in it?" "What shape do you think it will be?" "How can we make our pumpkin appear?" Then pass out "magic" pumpkin seeds for children to eat. Explain that these seeds will give them pretend magic power to see the pumpkin and to get inside of it. When everyone has a seed, say this chant together:
Abracadabra, pull you ear, eat this seed, and a pumpkin will appear. Poof!!

Have your children reach out from where they are sitting and "feel" the outside of the pumpkin. Talk about its texture and shape. Help children visualize the giant pumpkin that's inside the circle.

Next say, "But how can we get inside the pumpkin? I know, let's do a pumpkin dance." Stand up and join hands. While you dance around the "pumpkin," sing this song:

The Pumpkin Song
(Tune: "In and Out the Windows")
> *Go 'round and 'round the pumpkin.*
> *Go 'round and 'round the pumpkin.*
> *Go 'round and 'round the pumpkin*
> *To find the way inside!*

As this song is being sung, lead your children "inside" the pumpkin and have them explore it. Pass out a "magic seed" (a balloon) to each child, put on some music, and ask everyone to try to keep their seeds up in the air as they move to the music *and* stay inside the pumpkin.

When the music ends, tell your children that the magic is wearing off. Leave the balloons "inside" the pumpkin, get in a circle again, and sing "The Pumpkin Song" one more time to find your way *out*. Pass out another magic pumpkin seed for each child to eat. Explain that this seed will make the giant magic pumpkin disappear. This time chant:
Abracadabra, pull your ear, eat this seed, and the pumpkin will disappear. Poof!!

Remember
▪ Use these kinds of guided journeys as fun and relaxing breaks in your day. You don't need any props — just some mood music and your imaginative, whispering voice.
▪ If children are reluctant to participate, give them the choice to watch. Most often they will join in, in time.

BOOKS

Try other creative movement ideas and dramatic activities from these books.

▪ *Feeling Strong, Feeling Free: Movement Exploration for Young Children* by Molly Sullivan (NAEYC)

▪ *Music and Movement Improvisations* by Stecher, McElheny, and Greenwood (Macmillan)

▪ *Telling Stories Through Movement* by Margaret Dorain and Frances Gulland (Fearon)

ACTIVITY PLAN INDEX:
TWOS AND THREES

DEVELOPMENTAL AREAS AND SKILLS ENHANCED	Listening Skills	Creative Thinking	Music and Sound Concepts	Self-Expression	Autonomy and Self-Esteem	Social Interaction Skills	Cultural Awareness	Gross-Motor Skills	Fine-Motor Skills	Language Development	Logic and Reasoning Skills
2'S ACTIVITY PLANS											
SONG-CHART SINGING PAGE 38	■			■	■	■	■		■	■	
HUM A SONG WITH ME PAGE 39	■		■	■	■			■	■	■	■
WE'RE MUSICAL MOVERS! PAGE 40	■	■	■	■	■	■		■		■	
DANCING WITH BELLS PAGE 41	■		■	■	■		■	■			■
EASY DOES IT PAGE 42	■		■			■		■		■	
LOOK AT ME GO! PAGE 43		■		■	■			■	■		■
FALLING RAIN DANCE PAGE 44	■	■	■	■	■	■		■		■	■
FOOTLOOSE AND FANCY-FREE PAGE 45	■		■	■		■		■			
STREAMER "STICKS" PAGE 46	■	■	■	■		■	■	■	■		■
OUTDOOR PARACHUTE FUN PAGE 47	■	■		■	■	■	■	■	■		■
3'S ACTIVITY PLANS											
OUR FAVORITE HITS! PAGE 48	■	■		■	■	■	■	■	■		
MUSIC SHAPES, MUSIC PATTERNS PAGE 49	■	■	■	■	■	■			■	■	■
ROUTINE RHYMES PAGE 50	■				■				■	■	
MUSICAL FEELINGS PAGE 51	■	■	■	■	■				■	■	
DANCE AND SING FOR SPRING PAGE 52	■	■	■	■	■			■	■	■	■
WAYS TO GO PAGE 53		■		■	■		■	■		■	
THE WIND AND MY BALLOON PAGE 54		■		■	■	■			■	■	■
DANCE WITH THE WIND PAGE 55	■	■	■	■	■			■	■	■	■
HAVE A LIMBO PARTY! PAGE 56	■	■		■	■	■	■	■		■	■
THE BEAR WENT OVER THE MOUNTAIN PAGE 57	■	■		■	■	■		■	■	■	■

ACTIVITY PLAN INDEX:
FOURS AND FIVES

DEVELOPMENTAL AREAS AND SKILLS ENHANCED	Listening Skills	Creative Thinking	Music and Sound Concepts	Self-Expression	Autonomy and Self-Esteem	Social Interaction Skills	Cultural Awareness	Gross-Motor Skills	Fine-Motor Skills	Language Development	Logic and Reasoning Skills
4'S ACTIVITY PLANS											
WAKE THE EARTH WITH MUSIC! PAGE 58	■	■	■	■	■	■		■	■	■	■
RHYTHM AND RHYME PAGE 59	■	■	■	■	■			■	■	■	
WATER YOUR FEELINGS! PAGE 60	■		■	■	■	■	■	■		■	■
SHAKE A SOUND PAGE 61	■		■	■	■			■	■	■	
THE "I CAN" CAPE PAGE 62	■			■	■		■	■	■		■
MOVING IN PLACE PAGE 63	■			■	■	■	■	■			■
BEING BUBBLES PAGE 64	■	■		■	■	■	■	■		■	■
MY MIRROR AND I PAGE 65	■	■	■	■	■	■		■			
FROM CATERPILLARS TO BUTTERFLIES PAGE 66	■	■		■	■			■		■	■
WE'RE DANCING MACHINES! PAGE 67	■	■		■	■	■		■			
5'S ACTIVITY PLANS											
SHARING FAVORITE MUSIC FROM HOME PAGE 68	■		■		■	■	■	■			
STRIKE UP THE GADGET BAND! PAGE 69	■	■	■	■	■	■		■	■	■	■
SPONTANEOUS SOUNDS OF THE PLAYGROUND PAGE 70	■	■	■	■	■	■			■		
ORCHESTRATE A FAVORITE STORY PAGE 71	■	■	■			■	■		■	■	
LET'S HAVE A KAZOO PARADE! PAGE 72	■	■	■	■	■	■		■	■		■
COME-AND-GO PARTNERS PAGE 73	■	■		■	■	■	■	■			
THE DANCE OF THE FALLING LEAVES PAGE 74	■	■	■	■	■	■		■			■
MAGIC DANCING PAGE 75	■		■	■	■	■	■	■	■	■	■
MOVEMENT SCULPTURES PAGE 76	■	■		■	■	■		■		■	■
A MAGIC PUMPKIN JOURNEY PAGE 77	■	■		■	■		■		■	■	■

RESOURCES

Use the following resources to enhance your music and movement program. You'll find them in libraries and book or record stores, or contact the producer or publisher directly for ordering information. Consider sharing resources with other programs, too!

GREAT MUSIC FOR CHILDREN

▼ *All for Freedom* by Sweet Honey in the Rock (Music for Little People, P.O. Box 1460, Redway, CA 95560)

▼ *Bathtime Magic* by Joanie Bartels (Discovery Music, 5554 Calhoun Avenue, Van Nuys, CA 91401)

▼ *Birds, Beasts, Bugs, and Little Fishes* by Pete Seeger (Smithsonian/Folkways Records, Office of Folklife Programs, 955 L'Enfant Plaza, Suite 2600, Smithsonian Institution, Washington, DC 20560)

▼ *Color Me Wild* by Rory Block (Alcazam! Alcazar Productions, Inc., P.O. Box 429, Waterbury, VT 05676)

▼ *Ella Jenkins Live! At the Smithsonian* (video; Smithsonian/Folkways Records, distributed by Rounder Records, 1 Camp Street, Cambridge, MA 02140)

▼ *For Our Children* by Walt Disney Records (available at many record stores)

▼ *Granny, Will Your Dog Bite and Other Mountain Rhymes* by Gerald Milnes (Alfred A. Knopf)

▼ *I Know the Colors in the Rainbow* by Ella Jenkins (Educational Activities, Inc., P.O. Box 87, Baldwin, NY 11510)

▼ *Marcia Berman Sings Lullabies and Songs You Never Dreamed Were Lullabies* by Marcia Berman (Distributed by B/B Records, 570 N. Arden Blvd., Los Angeles, CA 90004)

▼ *Peace Is the World Smiling* (Music for Little People, P.O. Box 1460, Redway, CA 95560)

▼ *Piggyback Planet Songs for a Whole Earth* by Sally Rogers (Round River Records, 301 Jacob Street, Seekonk, MA 02771)

▼ *Shake It to the One That You Love the Best* by Cheryl Warren Mattox (Warren Mattox Productions, 3817 San Pablo Dam Road, #336, El Sobrante, CA 94803)

▼ *Shake Sugaree* by Taj Majal (Music for Little People, P.O. Box 1460, Redway, CA 95560)

▼ *Sillytime Magic* by Joanie Bartels (Discovery Music, 4130 Greenbush Avenue, Sherman Oaks, CA 91423)

▼ *Songs for the Whole Day* by Thomas Moore (Thomas Moore Records, 4600 Park Road, Suite 1000, Charlotte, NC 28209)

RESOURCE BOOKS FOR TEACHERS

▼ *Dance for Young Children: Finding the Magic in Movement* by Sue Stinson (American Alliance for Health, Physical Education)

▼ *Feeling Strong, Feeling Free: Movement Exploration for Young Children* by Molly Sullivan (NAEYC)

▼ *Hello World! Creative Development in Early Childhood Through Movement and Art* by Barbara Stewart Jones (Pitman Learning)

▼ *Leading Young Children to Music* by B. Joan Haines & Linda L. Gerber (Charles E. Merrill)

▼ *Music: A Way of Life for the Young Child* by Kathleen M. Bayless and Marjorie Ramsey (Mosby Co.)